This book belongs to:

Name:_____
Tel: _____
Email: _____

The Reseller
Inventory Log Book

Fast And Easy System To Keep Track Of Your Inventory Items.

Specially made for the Online Reseller

By
Queen Thrift

www.QueenThrift.com

Copyright © 2019 by Gianeska Publishing, Inc.

All rights reserved. No part of this publication may be reproduced, distributed, or transmitted in any form or by any means, including photocopying, recording, or other electronic or mechanical methods, without the prior written permission of the publisher, except in the case of brief quotations embodied in critical reviews and certain other noncommercial uses permitted by copyright law

Reseller Inventory Log
Some Tips

- **Date**. It's a good idea to write the date you are entering the items in the log. If you ever need to refer to an item by the date you can quickly jump to that section. Also, it will give you an idea of how long you have the item for. Good rule is to discount items sitting in your store for more than six months, unless they are seasonal. In such case you want to wait until the season comes to sell your items.

- **Flaws**.
  You want to under promise, and over deliver to your customers. You can avoid negative feedback and returns, by accurately disclosing any flaws in your items. Carefully test and inspect anything you put up for sale, and write it down so when you are listing, you can refer to this notes and include them in your listing. Make sure to photograph the flaws as well.

- **Sold On**.
  Crossing items off as they sell is a useful way to make sure we don't duplicate a listing. There are times when you think we still have an item in stock, when we don't. If you cross list to different platforms, this can help you make sure your inventory is synchronized.

- **Loc = Location**
  It's a good idea to stablish an inventory system early on so that you can grow into it. It can be as simple as having plastic bins numbered, and your items in it. For example, you have a clock for sale, and you put it in Bin A. In your listing description, you include "BinA". When it sells, you can quickly locate your item, saving you time and money. The less time you spend looking for your items to ship, the higher amount of profit you will make per hour.
  Spend some time refining this area, as you buy more and more items to sell, you will find it a lot easier to manage with an inventory system.

  Abbreviations used:
  PM: Poshmark
  EBY: eBay
  MER: Mercari
  Other: Any other marketplace you sell on. Facebook, LetGo, Offer Up, etc.
  LOC: Location of the item in your inventory.
  SKU#: Stock Keeping Unit. If you have an inventory system that uses this numbering system, this is where you would enter it. Otherwise leave it blank.

Date:_____   # Inventory Log

Brand:	Type:	Model:	Flaws:
Accessories:		Serial:	
Condition:	Color:	Listed: PM ___ EBY ___ MER___ Other:_____	Function:
Category:	Tested:	Cost:	Sold Price:	Loc: SKU#
Notes:		Date Acquired:	Sold on:	Profit:

Brand:	Type:	Model:	Flaws:
Accessories:		Serial:	
Condition:	Color:	Listed: PM ___ EBY ___ MER___ Other:_____	Function:
Category:	Tested:	Cost:	Sold Price:	Loc: SKU#
Notes:		Date Acquired:	Sold on:	Profit:

Brand:	Type:	Model:	Flaws:
Accessories:		Serial:	
Condition:	Color:	Listed: PM ___ EBY ___ MER___ Other:_____	Function:
Category:	Tested:	Cost:	Sold Price:	Loc: SKU#
Notes:		Date Acquired:	Sold on:	Profit:

Brand:	Type:	Model:	Flaws:
Accessories:		Serial:	
Condition:	Color:	Listed: PM ___ EBY ___ MER___ Other:_____	Function:
Category:	Tested:	Cost:	Sold Price:	Loc: SKU#
Notes:		Date Acquired:	Sold on:	Profit:

Date:_____ # Inventory Log

Brand:	Type:	Model:	Flaws:
Accessories:		Serial:	
Condition:	Color:	Listed: PM ___ EBY ___ MER___ Other:_____	Function:
Category:	Tested:	Cost:	Sold Price:	Loc:	SKU#
Notes:		Date Acquired:	Sold on:	Profit:

Brand:	Type:	Model:	Flaws:
Accessories:		Serial:	
Condition:	Color:	Listed: PM ___ EBY ___ MER___ Other:_____	Function:
Category:	Tested:	Cost:	Sold Price:	Loc:	SKU#
Notes:		Date Acquired:	Sold on:	Profit:

Brand:	Type:	Model:	Flaws:
Accessories:		Serial:	
Condition:	Color:	Listed: PM ___ EBY ___ MER___ Other:_____	Function:
Category:	Tested:	Cost:	Sold Price:	Loc:	SKU#
Notes:		Date Acquired:	Sold on:	Profit:

Brand:	Type:	Model:	Flaws:
Accessories:		Serial:	
Condition:	Color:	Listed: PM ___ EBY ___ MER___ Other:_____	Function:
Category:	Tested:	Cost:	Sold Price:	Loc:	SKU#
Notes:		Date Acquired:	Sold on:	Profit:

Date:_____ # Inventory Log

Brand:	Type:	Model:	Flaws:
Accessories:		Serial:	
Condition:	Color:	Listed: PM ___ EBY ___ MER___ Other:_____	Function:
Category:	Tested:	Cost:	Sold Price:	Loc: SKU#
Notes:		Date Acquired:	Sold on:	Profit:

Brand:	Type:	Model:	Flaws:
Accessories:		Serial:	
Condition:	Color:	Listed: PM ___ EBY ___ MER___ Other:_____	Function:
Category:	Tested:	Cost:	Sold Price:	Loc: SKU#
Notes:		Date Acquired:	Sold on:	Profit:

Brand:	Type:	Model:	Flaws:
Accessories:		Serial:	
Condition:	Color:	Listed: PM ___ EBY ___ MER___ Other:_____	Function:
Category:	Tested:	Cost:	Sold Price:	Loc: SKU#
Notes:		Date Acquired:	Sold on:	Profit:

Brand:	Type:	Model:	Flaws:
Accessories:		Serial:	
Condition:	Color:	Listed: PM ___ EBY ___ MER___ Other:_____	Function:
Category:	Tested:	Cost:	Sold Price:	Loc: SKU#
Notes:		Date Acquired:	Sold on:	Profit:

Date:_____ # Inventory Log

Brand:	Type:	Model:		Flaws:	
Accessories:		Serial:			
Condition:	Color:	Listed: PM ___ EBY ___ MER___ Other:_____		Function:	
Category:	Tested:	Cost:	Sold Price:	Loc:	SKU#
Notes:		Date Acquired:		Sold on:	Profit:

Brand:	Type:	Model:		Flaws:	
Accessories:		Serial:			
Condition:	Color:	Listed: PM ___ EBY ___ MER___ Other:_____		Function:	
Category:	Tested:	Cost:	Sold Price:	Loc:	SKU#
Notes:		Date Acquired:		Sold on:	Profit:

Brand:	Type:	Model:		Flaws:	
Accessories:		Serial:			
Condition:	Color:	Listed: PM ___ EBY ___ MER___ Other:_____		Function:	
Category:	Tested:	Cost:	Sold Price:	Loc:	SKU#
Notes:		Date Acquired:		Sold on:	Profit:

Brand:	Type:	Model:		Flaws:	
Accessories:		Serial:			
Condition:	Color:	Listed: PM ___ EBY ___ MER___ Other:_____		Function:	
Category:	Tested:	Cost:	Sold Price:	Loc:	SKU#
Notes:		Date Acquired:		Sold on:	Profit:

Date:_____ # Inventory Log

Brand:	Type:	Model:	Flaws:
Accessories:		Serial:	
Condition:	Color:	Listed: PM ___ EBY ___ MER___ Other:_____	Function:
Category:	Tested:	Cost:	Sold Price:	Loc: SKU#
Notes:		Date Acquired:	Sold on:	Profit:

Brand:	Type:	Model:	Flaws:
Accessories:		Serial:	
Condition:	Color:	Listed: PM ___ EBY ___ MER___ Other:_____	Function:
Category:	Tested:	Cost:	Sold Price:	Loc: SKU#
Notes:		Date Acquired:	Sold on:	Profit:

Brand:	Type:	Model:	Flaws:
Accessories:		Serial:	
Condition:	Color:	Listed: PM ___ EBY ___ MER___ Other:_____	Function:
Category:	Tested:	Cost:	Sold Price:	Loc: SKU#
Notes:		Date Acquired:	Sold on:	Profit:

Brand:	Type:	Model:	Flaws:
Accessories:		Serial:	
Condition:	Color:	Listed: PM ___ EBY ___ MER___ Other:_____	Function:
Category:	Tested:	Cost:	Sold Price:	Loc: SKU#
Notes:		Date Acquired:	Sold on:	Profit:

Date:_____ # Inventory Log

Brand:	Type:	Model:	Flaws:
Accessories:		Serial:	
Condition:	Color:	Listed: PM ___ EBY ___ MER___ Other:_____	Function:
Category:	Tested:	Cost:	Sold Price:	Loc: SKU#
Notes:		Date Acquired:	Sold on:	Profit:

Brand:	Type:	Model:	Flaws:
Accessories:		Serial:	
Condition:	Color:	Listed: PM ___ EBY ___ MER___ Other:_____	Function:
Category:	Tested:	Cost:	Sold Price:	Loc: SKU#
Notes:		Date Acquired:	Sold on:	Profit:

Brand:	Type:	Model:	Flaws:
Accessories:		Serial:	
Condition:	Color:	Listed: PM ___ EBY ___ MER___ Other:_____	Function:
Category:	Tested:	Cost:	Sold Price:	Loc: SKU#
Notes:		Date Acquired:	Sold on:	Profit:

Brand:	Type:	Model:	Flaws:
Accessories:		Serial:	
Condition:	Color:	Listed: PM ___ EBY ___ MER___ Other:_____	Function:
Category:	Tested:	Cost:	Sold Price:	Loc: SKU#
Notes:		Date Acquired:	Sold on:	Profit:

Date:_____ # Inventory Log

Brand:	Type:	Model:		Flaws:	
Accessories:		Serial:			
Condition:	Color:	Listed: PM ___ EBY ___ MER___ Other:_____		Function:	
Category:	Tested:	Cost:	Sold Price:	Loc: SKU#	
Notes:		Date Acquired:		Sold on:	Profit:

Brand:	Type:	Model:		Flaws:	
Accessories:		Serial:			
Condition:	Color:	Listed: PM ___ EBY ___ MER___ Other:_____		Function:	
Category:	Tested:	Cost:	Sold Price:	Loc: SKU#	
Notes:		Date Acquired:		Sold on:	Profit:

Brand:	Type:	Model:		Flaws:	
Accessories:		Serial:			
Condition:	Color:	Listed: PM ___ EBY ___ MER___ Other:_____		Function:	
Category:	Tested:	Cost:	Sold Price:	Loc: SKU#	
Notes:		Date Acquired:		Sold on:	Profit:

Brand:	Type:	Model:		Flaws:	
Accessories:		Serial:			
Condition:	Color:	Listed: PM ___ EBY ___ MER___ Other:_____		Function:	
Category:	Tested:	Cost:	Sold Price:	Loc: SKU#	
Notes:		Date Acquired:		Sold on:	Profit:

Date:_____   # Inventory Log

Brand:	Type:	Model:	Flaws:
Accessories:		Serial:	
Condition:	Color:	Listed: PM ___ EBY ___ MER___ Other:_____	Function:
Category:	Tested:	Cost:	Sold Price:	Loc: SKU#
Notes:		Date Acquired:	Sold on:	Profit:

Brand:	Type:	Model:	Flaws:
Accessories:		Serial:	
Condition:	Color:	Listed: PM ___ EBY ___ MER___ Other:_____	Function:
Category:	Tested:	Cost:	Sold Price:	Loc: SKU#
Notes:		Date Acquired:	Sold on:	Profit:

Brand:	Type:	Model:	Flaws:
Accessories:		Serial:	
Condition:	Color:	Listed: PM ___ EBY ___ MER___ Other:_____	Function:
Category:	Tested:	Cost:	Sold Price:	Loc: SKU#
Notes:		Date Acquired:	Sold on:	Profit:

Brand:	Type:	Model:	Flaws:
Accessories:		Serial:	
Condition:	Color:	Listed: PM ___ EBY ___ MER___ Other:_____	Function:
Category:	Tested:	Cost:	Sold Price:	Loc: SKU#
Notes:		Date Acquired:	Sold on:	Profit:

Date:_____ # Inventory Log

Brand:	Type:	Model:	Flaws:
Accessories:		Serial:	
Condition:	Color:	Listed: PM ___ EBY ___ MER___ Other:_____	Function:
Category:	Tested:	Cost:	Sold Price:	Loc: SKU#
Notes:		Date Acquired:	Sold on:	Profit:

Brand:	Type:	Model:	Flaws:
Accessories:		Serial:	
Condition:	Color:	Listed: PM ___ EBY ___ MER___ Other:_____	Function:
Category:	Tested:	Cost:	Sold Price:	Loc: SKU#
Notes:		Date Acquired:	Sold on:	Profit:

Brand:	Type:	Model:	Flaws:
Accessories:		Serial:	
Condition:	Color:	Listed: PM ___ EBY ___ MER___ Other:_____	Function:
Category:	Tested:	Cost:	Sold Price:	Loc: SKU#
Notes:		Date Acquired:	Sold on:	Profit:

Brand:	Type:	Model:	Flaws:
Accessories:		Serial:	
Condition:	Color:	Listed: PM ___ EBY ___ MER___ Other:_____	Function:
Category:	Tested:	Cost:	Sold Price:	Loc: SKU#
Notes:		Date Acquired:	Sold on:	Profit:

Date:_____ # Inventory Log

Brand:	Type:	Model:	Flaws:
Accessories:		Serial:	
Condition:	Color:	Listed: PM ___ EBY ___ MER___ Other:_____	Function:
Category:	Tested:	Cost:	Sold Price:	Loc:	SKU#
Notes:		Date Acquired:	Sold on:	Profit:

Brand:	Type:	Model:	Flaws:
Accessories:		Serial:	
Condition:	Color:	Listed: PM ___ EBY ___ MER___ Other:_____	Function:
Category:	Tested:	Cost:	Sold Price:	Loc:	SKU#
Notes:		Date Acquired:	Sold on:	Profit:

Brand:	Type:	Model:	Flaws:
Accessories:		Serial:	
Condition:	Color:	Listed: PM ___ EBY ___ MER___ Other:_____	Function:
Category:	Tested:	Cost:	Sold Price:	Loc:	SKU#
Notes:		Date Acquired:	Sold on:	Profit:

Brand:	Type:	Model:	Flaws:
Accessories:		Serial:	
Condition:	Color:	Listed: PM ___ EBY ___ MER___ Other:_____	Function:
Category:	Tested:	Cost:	Sold Price:	Loc:	SKU#
Notes:		Date Acquired:	Sold on:	Profit:

Date:_____ # Inventory Log

Brand:	Type:	Model:	Flaws:
Accessories:		Serial:	
Condition:	Color:	Listed: PM ___ EBY ___ MER___ Other:_____	Function:
Category:	Tested:	Cost:	Sold Price:	Loc: SKU#
Notes:		Date Acquired:	Sold on:	Profit:

Brand:	Type:	Model:	Flaws:
Accessories:		Serial:	
Condition:	Color:	Listed: PM ___ EBY ___ MER___ Other:_____	Function:
Category:	Tested:	Cost:	Sold Price:	Loc: SKU#
Notes:		Date Acquired:	Sold on:	Profit:

Brand:	Type:	Model:	Flaws:
Accessories:		Serial:	
Condition:	Color:	Listed: PM ___ EBY ___ MER___ Other:_____	Function:
Category:	Tested:	Cost:	Sold Price:	Loc: SKU#
Notes:		Date Acquired:	Sold on:	Profit:

Brand:	Type:	Model:	Flaws:
Accessories:		Serial:	
Condition:	Color:	Listed: PM ___ EBY ___ MER___ Other:_____	Function:
Category:	Tested:	Cost:	Sold Price:	Loc: SKU#
Notes:		Date Acquired:	Sold on:	Profit:

Date:_____ # Inventory Log

Brand:	Type:	Model:	Flaws:
Accessories:		Serial:	
Condition:	Color:	Listed: PM ___ EBY ___ MER___ Other:_____	Function:
Category:	Tested:	Cost:	Sold Price:	Loc:	SKU#
Notes:		Date Acquired:	Sold on:	Profit:

Brand:	Type:	Model:	Flaws:
Accessories:		Serial:	
Condition:	Color:	Listed: PM ___ EBY ___ MER___ Other:_____	Function:
Category:	Tested:	Cost:	Sold Price:	Loc:	SKU#
Notes:		Date Acquired:	Sold on:	Profit:

Brand:	Type:	Model:	Flaws:
Accessories:		Serial:	
Condition:	Color:	Listed: PM ___ EBY ___ MER___ Other:_____	Function:
Category:	Tested:	Cost:	Sold Price:	Loc:	SKU#
Notes:		Date Acquired:	Sold on:	Profit:

Brand:	Type:	Model:	Flaws:
Accessories:		Serial:	
Condition:	Color:	Listed: PM ___ EBY ___ MER___ Other:_____	Function:
Category:	Tested:	Cost:	Sold Price:	Loc:	SKU#
Notes:		Date Acquired:	Sold on:	Profit:

Date:_____ # Inventory Log

Brand:	Type:	Model:	Flaws:
Accessories:		Serial:	
Condition:	Color:	Listed: PM ___ EBY ___ MER___ Other:_____	Function:
Category:	Tested:	Cost:	Sold Price:	Loc: SKU#
Notes:		Date Acquired:	Sold on:	Profit:

Brand:	Type:	Model:	Flaws:
Accessories:		Serial:	
Condition:	Color:	Listed: PM ___ EBY ___ MER___ Other:_____	Function:
Category:	Tested:	Cost:	Sold Price:	Loc: SKU#
Notes:		Date Acquired:	Sold on:	Profit:

Brand:	Type:	Model:	Flaws:
Accessories:		Serial:	
Condition:	Color:	Listed: PM ___ EBY ___ MER___ Other:_____	Function:
Category:	Tested:	Cost:	Sold Price:	Loc: SKU#
Notes:		Date Acquired:	Sold on:	Profit:

Brand:	Type:	Model:	Flaws:
Accessories:		Serial:	
Condition:	Color:	Listed: PM ___ EBY ___ MER___ Other:_____	Function:
Category:	Tested:	Cost:	Sold Price:	Loc: SKU#
Notes:		Date Acquired:	Sold on:	Profit:

Inventory Log

Date:_____

Brand:	Type:	Model:		Flaws:	
Accessories:		Serial:			
Condition:	Color:	Listed: PM ___ EBY ___ MER___ Other:_____		Function:	
Category:	Tested:	Cost:	Sold Price:	Loc: SKU#	
Notes:		Date Acquired:		Sold on:	Profit:

Brand:	Type:	Model:		Flaws:	
Accessories:		Serial:			
Condition:	Color:	Listed: PM ___ EBY ___ MER___ Other:_____		Function:	
Category:	Tested:	Cost:	Sold Price:	Loc: SKU#	
Notes:		Date Acquired:		Sold on:	Profit:

Brand:	Type:	Model:		Flaws:	
Accessories:		Serial:			
Condition:	Color:	Listed: PM ___ EBY ___ MER___ Other:_____		Function:	
Category:	Tested:	Cost:	Sold Price:	Loc: SKU#	
Notes:		Date Acquired:		Sold on:	Profit:

Brand:	Type:	Model:		Flaws:	
Accessories:		Serial:			
Condition:	Color:	Listed: PM ___ EBY ___ MER___ Other:_____		Function:	
Category:	Tested:	Cost:	Sold Price:	Loc: SKU#	
Notes:		Date Acquired:		Sold on:	Profit:

Date:_____ # Inventory Log

Brand:	Type:	Model:		Flaws:	
Accessories:		Serial:			
Condition:	Color:	Listed: PM ___ EBY ___ MER___ Other:_____		Function:	
Category:	Tested:	Cost:	Sold Price:	Loc:	SKU#
Notes:		Date Acquired:		Sold on:	Profit:

Brand:	Type:	Model:		Flaws:	
Accessories:		Serial:			
Condition:	Color:	Listed: PM ___ EBY ___ MER___ Other:_____		Function:	
Category:	Tested:	Cost:	Sold Price:	Loc:	SKU#
Notes:		Date Acquired:		Sold on:	Profit:

Brand:	Type:	Model:		Flaws:	
Accessories:		Serial:			
Condition:	Color:	Listed: PM ___ EBY ___ MER___ Other:_____		Function:	
Category:	Tested:	Cost:	Sold Price:	Loc:	SKU#
Notes:		Date Acquired:		Sold on:	Profit:

Brand:	Type:	Model:		Flaws:	
Accessories:		Serial:			
Condition:	Color:	Listed: PM ___ EBY ___ MER___ Other:_____		Function:	
Category:	Tested:	Cost:	Sold Price:	Loc:	SKU#
Notes:		Date Acquired:		Sold on:	Profit:

Date:_____ # Inventory Log

Brand:	Type:	Model:		Flaws:	
Accessories:		Serial:			
Condition:	Color:	Listed: PM ___ EBY ___ MER ___ Other:_____		Function:	
Category:	Tested:	Cost:	Sold Price:	Loc:	SKU#
Notes:		Date Acquired:		Sold on:	Profit:

Brand:	Type:	Model:		Flaws:	
Accessories:		Serial:			
Condition:	Color:	Listed: PM ___ EBY ___ MER ___ Other:_____		Function:	
Category:	Tested:	Cost:	Sold Price:	Loc:	SKU#
Notes:		Date Acquired:		Sold on:	Profit:

Brand:	Type:	Model:		Flaws:	
Accessories:		Serial:			
Condition:	Color:	Listed: PM ___ EBY ___ MER ___ Other:_____		Function:	
Category:	Tested:	Cost:	Sold Price:	Loc:	SKU#
Notes:		Date Acquired:		Sold on:	Profit:

Brand:	Type:	Model:		Flaws:	
Accessories:		Serial:			
Condition:	Color:	Listed: PM ___ EBY ___ MER ___ Other:_____		Function:	
Category:	Tested:	Cost:	Sold Price:	Loc:	SKU#
Notes:		Date Acquired:		Sold on:	Profit:

Date:_____   # Inventory Log

Brand:	Type:	Model:	Flaws:
Accessories:		Serial:	
Condition:	Color:	Listed: PM ___ EBY ___ MER___ Other:_____	Function:
Category:	Tested:	Cost:	Sold Price:	Loc: SKU#
Notes:		Date Acquired:	Sold on:	Profit:

Brand:	Type:	Model:	Flaws:
Accessories:		Serial:	
Condition:	Color:	Listed: PM ___ EBY ___ MER___ Other:_____	Function:
Category:	Tested:	Cost:	Sold Price:	Loc: SKU#
Notes:		Date Acquired:	Sold on:	Profit:

Brand:	Type:	Model:	Flaws:
Accessories:		Serial:	
Condition:	Color:	Listed: PM ___ EBY ___ MER___ Other:_____	Function:
Category:	Tested:	Cost:	Sold Price:	Loc: SKU#
Notes:		Date Acquired:	Sold on:	Profit:

Brand:	Type:	Model:	Flaws:
Accessories:		Serial:	
Condition:	Color:	Listed: PM ___ EBY ___ MER___ Other:_____	Function:
Category:	Tested:	Cost:	Sold Price:	Loc: SKU#
Notes:		Date Acquired:	Sold on:	Profit:

Date:_____   # Inventory Log

Brand:	Type:	Model:	Flaws:
Accessories:		Serial:	
Condition:	Color:	Listed: PM ___ EBY ___ MER___ Other:_____	Function:
Category:	Tested:	Cost:	Sold Price:	Loc: SKU#
Notes:		Date Acquired:	Sold on:	Profit:

Brand:	Type:	Model:	Flaws:
Accessories:		Serial:	
Condition:	Color:	Listed: PM ___ EBY ___ MER___ Other:_____	Function:
Category:	Tested:	Cost:	Sold Price:	Loc: SKU#
Notes:		Date Acquired:	Sold on:	Profit:

Brand:	Type:	Model:	Flaws:
Accessories:		Serial:	
Condition:	Color:	Listed: PM ___ EBY ___ MER___ Other:_____	Function:
Category:	Tested:	Cost:	Sold Price:	Loc: SKU#
Notes:		Date Acquired:	Sold on:	Profit:

Brand:	Type:	Model:	Flaws:
Accessories:		Serial:	
Condition:	Color:	Listed: PM ___ EBY ___ MER___ Other:_____	Function:
Category:	Tested:	Cost:	Sold Price:	Loc: SKU#
Notes:		Date Acquired:	Sold on:	Profit:

Date:_____ # Inventory Log

Brand:	Type:	Model:	Flaws:
Accessories:		Serial:	
Condition:	Color:	Listed: PM ___ EBY ___ MER___ Other:_____	Function:
Category:	Tested:	Cost:	Sold Price:	Loc: SKU#
Notes:		Date Acquired:	Sold on:	Profit:

Brand:	Type:	Model:	Flaws:
Accessories:		Serial:	
Condition:	Color:	Listed: PM ___ EBY ___ MER___ Other:_____	Function:
Category:	Tested:	Cost:	Sold Price:	Loc: SKU#
Notes:		Date Acquired:	Sold on:	Profit:

Brand:	Type:	Model:	Flaws:
Accessories:		Serial:	
Condition:	Color:	Listed: PM ___ EBY ___ MER___ Other:_____	Function:
Category:	Tested:	Cost:	Sold Price:	Loc: SKU#
Notes:		Date Acquired:	Sold on:	Profit:

Brand:	Type:	Model:	Flaws:
Accessories:		Serial:	
Condition:	Color:	Listed: PM ___ EBY ___ MER___ Other:_____	Function:
Category:	Tested:	Cost:	Sold Price:	Loc: SKU#
Notes:		Date Acquired:	Sold on:	Profit:

Date:_____ # Inventory Log

Brand:	Type:	Model:		Flaws:	
Accessories:		Serial:			
Condition:	Color:	Listed: PM ___ EBY ___ MER___ Other:_____		Function:	
Category:	Tested:	Cost:	Sold Price:	Loc:	SKU#
Notes:		Date Acquired:		Sold on:	Profit:

Brand:	Type:	Model:		Flaws:	
Accessories:		Serial:			
Condition:	Color:	Listed: PM ___ EBY ___ MER___ Other:_____		Function:	
Category:	Tested:	Cost:	Sold Price:	Loc:	SKU#
Notes:		Date Acquired:		Sold on:	Profit:

Brand:	Type:	Model:		Flaws:	
Accessories:		Serial:			
Condition:	Color:	Listed: PM ___ EBY ___ MER___ Other:_____		Function:	
Category:	Tested:	Cost:	Sold Price:	Loc:	SKU#
Notes:		Date Acquired:		Sold on:	Profit:

Brand:	Type:	Model:		Flaws:	
Accessories:		Serial:			
Condition:	Color:	Listed: PM ___ EBY ___ MER___ Other:_____		Function:	
Category:	Tested:	Cost:	Sold Price:	Loc:	SKU#
Notes:		Date Acquired:		Sold on:	Profit:

Date:_____   # Inventory Log

Brand:	Type:	Model:		Flaws:	
Accessories:		Serial:			
Condition:	Color:	Listed: PM ___ EBY ___ MER___ Other:_____		Function:	
Category:	Tested:	Cost:	Sold Price:	Loc: SKU#	
Notes:		Date Acquired:		Sold on:	Profit:

Brand:	Type:	Model:		Flaws:	
Accessories:		Serial:			
Condition:	Color:	Listed: PM ___ EBY ___ MER___ Other:_____		Function:	
Category:	Tested:	Cost:	Sold Price:	Loc: SKU#	
Notes:		Date Acquired:		Sold on:	Profit:

Brand:	Type:	Model:		Flaws:	
Accessories:		Serial:			
Condition:	Color:	Listed: PM ___ EBY ___ MER___ Other:_____		Function:	
Category:	Tested:	Cost:	Sold Price:	Loc: SKU#	
Notes:		Date Acquired:		Sold on:	Profit:

Brand:	Type:	Model:		Flaws:	
Accessories:		Serial:			
Condition:	Color:	Listed: PM ___ EBY ___ MER___ Other:_____		Function:	
Category:	Tested:	Cost:	Sold Price:	Loc: SKU#	
Notes:		Date Acquired:		Sold on:	Profit:

Date:_____

Inventory Log

Brand:	Type:	Model:		Flaws:
Accessories:		Serial:		
Condition:	Color:	Listed: PM ___ EBY ___ MER___ Other:_____		Function:
Category:	Tested:	Cost:	Sold Price:	Loc: SKU#
Notes:		Date Acquired:	Sold on:	Profit:

Brand:	Type:	Model:		Flaws:
Accessories:		Serial:		
Condition:	Color:	Listed: PM ___ EBY ___ MER___ Other:_____		Function:
Category:	Tested:	Cost:	Sold Price:	Loc: SKU#
Notes:		Date Acquired:	Sold on:	Profit:

Brand:	Type:	Model:		Flaws:
Accessories:		Serial:		
Condition:	Color:	Listed: PM ___ EBY ___ MER___ Other:_____		Function:
Category:	Tested:	Cost:	Sold Price:	Loc: SKU#
Notes:		Date Acquired:	Sold on:	Profit:

Brand:	Type:	Model:		Flaws:
Accessories:		Serial:		
Condition:	Color:	Listed: PM ___ EBY ___ MER___ Other:_____		Function:
Category:	Tested:	Cost:	Sold Price:	Loc: SKU#
Notes:		Date Acquired:	Sold on:	Profit:

Date:_____ **Inventory Log**

Brand:	Type:	Model:	Flaws:
Accessories:		Serial:	
Condition:	Color:	Listed: PM ___ EBY ___ MER___ Other:_____	Function:
Category:	Tested:	Cost:	Sold Price:	Loc: SKU#
Notes:		Date Acquired:	Sold on:	Profit:

Brand:	Type:	Model:	Flaws:
Accessories:		Serial:	
Condition:	Color:	Listed: PM ___ EBY ___ MER___ Other:_____	Function:
Category:	Tested:	Cost:	Sold Price:	Loc: SKU#
Notes:		Date Acquired:	Sold on:	Profit:

Brand:	Type:	Model:	Flaws:
Accessories:		Serial:	
Condition:	Color:	Listed: PM ___ EBY ___ MER___ Other:_____	Function:
Category:	Tested:	Cost:	Sold Price:	Loc: SKU#
Notes:		Date Acquired:	Sold on:	Profit:

Brand:	Type:	Model:	Flaws:
Accessories:		Serial:	
Condition:	Color:	Listed: PM ___ EBY ___ MER___ Other:_____	Function:
Category:	Tested:	Cost:	Sold Price:	Loc: SKU#
Notes:		Date Acquired:	Sold on:	Profit:

Date:_____

Inventory Log

Brand:	Type:	Model:		Flaws:	
Accessories:		Serial:			
Condition:	Color:	Listed: PM ___ EBY ___ MER___ Other:_____		Function:	
Category:	Tested:	Cost:	Sold Price:	Loc:	SKU#
Notes:		Date Acquired:		Sold on:	Profit:

Brand:	Type:	Model:		Flaws:	
Accessories:		Serial:			
Condition:	Color:	Listed: PM ___ EBY ___ MER___ Other:_____		Function:	
Category:	Tested:	Cost:	Sold Price:	Loc:	SKU#
Notes:		Date Acquired:		Sold on:	Profit:

Brand:	Type:	Model:		Flaws:	
Accessories:		Serial:			
Condition:	Color:	Listed: PM ___ EBY ___ MER___ Other:_____		Function:	
Category:	Tested:	Cost:	Sold Price:	Loc:	SKU#
Notes:		Date Acquired:		Sold on:	Profit:

Brand:	Type:	Model:		Flaws:	
Accessories:		Serial:			
Condition:	Color:	Listed: PM ___ EBY ___ MER___ Other:_____		Function:	
Category:	Tested:	Cost:	Sold Price:	Loc:	SKU#
Notes:		Date Acquired:		Sold on:	Profit:

Date:_____ # Inventory Log

Brand:	Type:	Model:	Flaws:
Accessories:		Serial:	
Condition:	Color:	Listed: PM ___ EBY ___ MER___ Other:_____	Function:
Category:	Tested:	Cost:	Sold Price:	Loc: SKU#
Notes:		Date Acquired:	Sold on:	Profit:

Brand:	Type:	Model:	Flaws:
Accessories:		Serial:	
Condition:	Color:	Listed: PM ___ EBY ___ MER___ Other:_____	Function:
Category:	Tested:	Cost:	Sold Price:	Loc: SKU#
Notes:		Date Acquired:	Sold on:	Profit:

Brand:	Type:	Model:	Flaws:
Accessories:		Serial:	
Condition:	Color:	Listed: PM ___ EBY ___ MER___ Other:_____	Function:
Category:	Tested:	Cost:	Sold Price:	Loc: SKU#
Notes:		Date Acquired:	Sold on:	Profit:

Brand:	Type:	Model:	Flaws:
Accessories:		Serial:	
Condition:	Color:	Listed: PM ___ EBY ___ MER___ Other:_____	Function:
Category:	Tested:	Cost:	Sold Price:	Loc: SKU#
Notes:		Date Acquired:	Sold on:	Profit:

Date:_____   # Inventory Log

Brand:	Type:	Model:		Flaws:	
Accessories:		Serial:			
Condition:	Color:	Listed: PM ___ EBY ___ MER___ Other:_____		Function:	
Category:	Tested:	Cost:	Sold Price:	Loc: SKU#	
Notes:		Date Acquired:		Sold on:	Profit:

Brand:	Type:	Model:		Flaws:	
Accessories:		Serial:			
Condition:	Color:	Listed: PM ___ EBY ___ MER___ Other:_____		Function:	
Category:	Tested:	Cost:	Sold Price:	Loc: SKU#	
Notes:		Date Acquired:		Sold on:	Profit:

Brand:	Type:	Model:		Flaws:	
Accessories:		Serial:			
Condition:	Color:	Listed: PM ___ EBY ___ MER___ Other:_____		Function:	
Category:	Tested:	Cost:	Sold Price:	Loc: SKU#	
Notes:		Date Acquired:		Sold on:	Profit:

Brand:	Type:	Model:		Flaws:	
Accessories:		Serial:			
Condition:	Color:	Listed: PM ___ EBY ___ MER___ Other:_____		Function:	
Category:	Tested:	Cost:	Sold Price:	Loc: SKU#	
Notes:		Date Acquired:		Sold on:	Profit:

Date:_____   # Inventory Log

Brand:	Type:	Model:	Flaws:
Accessories:		Serial:	
Condition:	Color:	Listed: PM ___ EBY ___ MER___ Other:_____	Function:
Category:	Tested:	Cost:	Sold Price:	Loc:	SKU#
Notes:		Date Acquired:	Sold on:	Profit:

Brand:	Type:	Model:	Flaws:
Accessories:		Serial:	
Condition:	Color:	Listed: PM ___ EBY ___ MER___ Other:_____	Function:
Category:	Tested:	Cost:	Sold Price:	Loc:	SKU#
Notes:		Date Acquired:	Sold on:	Profit:

Brand:	Type:	Model:	Flaws:
Accessories:		Serial:	
Condition:	Color:	Listed: PM ___ EBY ___ MER___ Other:_____	Function:
Category:	Tested:	Cost:	Sold Price:	Loc:	SKU#
Notes:		Date Acquired:	Sold on:	Profit:

Brand:	Type:	Model:	Flaws:
Accessories:		Serial:	
Condition:	Color:	Listed: PM ___ EBY ___ MER___ Other:_____	Function:
Category:	Tested:	Cost:	Sold Price:	Loc:	SKU#
Notes:		Date Acquired:	Sold on:	Profit:

Date:_____ # Inventory Log

Brand:	Type:	Model:		Flaws:	
Accessories:		Serial:			
Condition:	Color:	Listed: PM ___ EBY ___ MER___ Other:_____		Function:	
Category:	Tested:	Cost:	Sold Price:	Loc: SKU#	
Notes:		Date Acquired:		Sold on:	Profit:

Brand:	Type:	Model:		Flaws:	
Accessories:		Serial:			
Condition:	Color:	Listed: PM ___ EBY ___ MER___ Other:_____		Function:	
Category:	Tested:	Cost:	Sold Price:	Loc: SKU#	
Notes:		Date Acquired:		Sold on:	Profit:

Brand:	Type:	Model:		Flaws:	
Accessories:		Serial:			
Condition:	Color:	Listed: PM ___ EBY ___ MER___ Other:_____		Function:	
Category:	Tested:	Cost:	Sold Price:	Loc: SKU#	
Notes:		Date Acquired:		Sold on:	Profit:

Brand:	Type:	Model:		Flaws:	
Accessories:		Serial:			
Condition:	Color:	Listed: PM ___ EBY ___ MER___ Other:_____		Function:	
Category:	Tested:	Cost:	Sold Price:	Loc: SKU#	
Notes:		Date Acquired:		Sold on:	Profit:

Date:_____ # Inventory Log

Brand:	Type:	Model:		Flaws:	
Accessories:		Serial:			
Condition:	Color:	Listed: PM ___ EBY ___ MER___ Other:_____		Function:	
Category:	Tested:	Cost:	Sold Price:	Loc:	SKU#
Notes:		Date Acquired:		Sold on:	Profit:

Brand:	Type:	Model:		Flaws:	
Accessories:		Serial:			
Condition:	Color:	Listed: PM ___ EBY ___ MER___ Other:_____		Function:	
Category:	Tested:	Cost:	Sold Price:	Loc:	SKU#
Notes:		Date Acquired:		Sold on:	Profit:

Brand:	Type:	Model:		Flaws:	
Accessories:		Serial:			
Condition:	Color:	Listed: PM ___ EBY ___ MER___ Other:_____		Function:	
Category:	Tested:	Cost:	Sold Price:	Loc:	SKU#
Notes:		Date Acquired:		Sold on:	Profit:

Brand:	Type:	Model:		Flaws:	
Accessories:		Serial:			
Condition:	Color:	Listed: PM ___ EBY ___ MER___ Other:_____		Function:	
Category:	Tested:	Cost:	Sold Price:	Loc:	SKU#
Notes:		Date Acquired:		Sold on:	Profit:

Date:_____   # Inventory Log

Brand:	Type:	Model:		Flaws:	
Accessories:		Serial:			
Condition:	Color:	Listed: PM ___ EBY ___ MER___ Other:_____		Function:	
Category:	Tested:	Cost:	Sold Price:	Loc:	SKU#
Notes:		Date Acquired:		Sold on:	Profit:

Brand:	Type:	Model:		Flaws:	
Accessories:		Serial:			
Condition:	Color:	Listed: PM ___ EBY ___ MER___ Other:_____		Function:	
Category:	Tested:	Cost:	Sold Price:	Loc:	SKU#
Notes:		Date Acquired:		Sold on:	Profit:

Brand:	Type:	Model:		Flaws:	
Accessories:		Serial:			
Condition:	Color:	Listed: PM ___ EBY ___ MER___ Other:_____		Function:	
Category:	Tested:	Cost:	Sold Price:	Loc:	SKU#
Notes:		Date Acquired:		Sold on:	Profit:

Brand:	Type:	Model:		Flaws:	
Accessories:		Serial:			
Condition:	Color:	Listed: PM ___ EBY ___ MER___ Other:_____		Function:	
Category:	Tested:	Cost:	Sold Price:	Loc:	SKU#
Notes:		Date Acquired:		Sold on:	Profit:

Date:_____   # Inventory Log

Brand:	Type:	Model:	Flaws:
Accessories:		Serial:	
Condition:	Color:	Listed: PM ___ EBY ___ MER___ Other:_____	Function:
Category:	Tested:	Cost:	Sold Price:	Loc: SKU#
Notes:		Date Acquired:	Sold on:	Profit:

Brand:	Type:	Model:	Flaws:
Accessories:		Serial:	
Condition:	Color:	Listed: PM ___ EBY ___ MER___ Other:_____	Function:
Category:	Tested:	Cost:	Sold Price:	Loc: SKU#
Notes:		Date Acquired:	Sold on:	Profit:

Brand:	Type:	Model:	Flaws:
Accessories:		Serial:	
Condition:	Color:	Listed: PM ___ EBY ___ MER___ Other:_____	Function:
Category:	Tested:	Cost:	Sold Price:	Loc: SKU#
Notes:		Date Acquired:	Sold on:	Profit:

Brand:	Type:	Model:	Flaws:
Accessories:		Serial:	
Condition:	Color:	Listed: PM ___ EBY ___ MER___ Other:_____	Function:
Category:	Tested:	Cost:	Sold Price:	Loc: SKU#
Notes:		Date Acquired:	Sold on:	Profit:

Date:_____ # Inventory Log

Brand:	Type:	Model:		Flaws:	
Accessories:		Serial:			
Condition:	Color:	Listed: PM ___ EBY ___ MER___ Other:_____		Function:	
Category:	Tested:	Cost:	Sold Price:	Loc: SKU#	
Notes:		Date Acquired:		Sold on:	Profit:

Brand:	Type:	Model:		Flaws:	
Accessories:		Serial:			
Condition:	Color:	Listed: PM ___ EBY ___ MER___ Other:_____		Function:	
Category:	Tested:	Cost:	Sold Price:	Loc: SKU#	
Notes:		Date Acquired:		Sold on:	Profit:

Brand:	Type:	Model:		Flaws:	
Accessories:		Serial:			
Condition:	Color:	Listed: PM ___ EBY ___ MER___ Other:_____		Function:	
Category:	Tested:	Cost:	Sold Price:	Loc: SKU#	
Notes:		Date Acquired:		Sold on:	Profit:

Brand:	Type:	Model:		Flaws:	
Accessories:		Serial:			
Condition:	Color:	Listed: PM ___ EBY ___ MER___ Other:_____		Function:	
Category:	Tested:	Cost:	Sold Price:	Loc: SKU#	
Notes:		Date Acquired:		Sold on:	Profit:

Date:_____ # Inventory Log

Brand:	Type:	Model:	Flaws:
Accessories:		Serial:	
Condition:	Color:	Listed: PM ___ EBY ___ MER___ Other:_____	Function:
Category:	Tested:	Cost:	Sold Price:	Loc: SKU#
Notes:		Date Acquired:	Sold on:	Profit:

Brand:	Type:	Model:	Flaws:
Accessories:		Serial:	
Condition:	Color:	Listed: PM ___ EBY ___ MER___ Other:_____	Function:
Category:	Tested:	Cost:	Sold Price:	Loc: SKU#
Notes:		Date Acquired:	Sold on:	Profit:

Brand:	Type:	Model:	Flaws:
Accessories:		Serial:	
Condition:	Color:	Listed: PM ___ EBY ___ MER___ Other:_____	Function:
Category:	Tested:	Cost:	Sold Price:	Loc: SKU#
Notes:		Date Acquired:	Sold on:	Profit:

Brand:	Type:	Model:	Flaws:
Accessories:		Serial:	
Condition:	Color:	Listed: PM ___ EBY ___ MER___ Other:_____	Function:
Category:	Tested:	Cost:	Sold Price:	Loc: SKU#
Notes:		Date Acquired:	Sold on:	Profit:

Date:_____ # Inventory Log

Brand:	Type:	Model:		Flaws:	
Accessories:		Serial:			
Condition:	Color:	Listed: PM ___ EBY ___ MER___ Other:_____		Function:	
Category:	Tested:	Cost:	Sold Price:	Loc: SKU#	
Notes:		Date Acquired:		Sold on:	Profit:

Brand:	Type:	Model:		Flaws:	
Accessories:		Serial:			
Condition:	Color:	Listed: PM ___ EBY ___ MER___ Other:_____		Function:	
Category:	Tested:	Cost:	Sold Price:	Loc: SKU#	
Notes:		Date Acquired:		Sold on:	Profit:

Brand:	Type:	Model:		Flaws:	
Accessories:		Serial:			
Condition:	Color:	Listed: PM ___ EBY ___ MER___ Other:_____		Function:	
Category:	Tested:	Cost:	Sold Price:	Loc: SKU#	
Notes:		Date Acquired:		Sold on:	Profit:

Brand:	Type:	Model:		Flaws:	
Accessories:		Serial:			
Condition:	Color:	Listed: PM ___ EBY ___ MER___ Other:_____		Function:	
Category:	Tested:	Cost:	Sold Price:	Loc: SKU#	
Notes:		Date Acquired:		Sold on:	Profit:

Date:_____ # Inventory Log

Brand:	Type:	Model:	Flaws:
Accessories:		Serial:	
Condition:	Color:	Listed: PM ___ EBY ___ MER___ Other:_____	Function:
Category:	Tested:	Cost:	Sold Price:	Loc: SKU#
Notes:		Date Acquired:	Sold on:	Profit:

Brand:	Type:	Model:	Flaws:
Accessories:		Serial:	
Condition:	Color:	Listed: PM ___ EBY ___ MER___ Other:_____	Function:
Category:	Tested:	Cost:	Sold Price:	Loc: SKU#
Notes:		Date Acquired:	Sold on:	Profit:

Brand:	Type:	Model:	Flaws:
Accessories:		Serial:	
Condition:	Color:	Listed: PM ___ EBY ___ MER___ Other:_____	Function:
Category:	Tested:	Cost:	Sold Price:	Loc: SKU#
Notes:		Date Acquired:	Sold on:	Profit:

Brand:	Type:	Model:	Flaws:
Accessories:		Serial:	
Condition:	Color:	Listed: PM ___ EBY ___ MER___ Other:_____	Function:
Category:	Tested:	Cost:	Sold Price:	Loc: SKU#
Notes:		Date Acquired:	Sold on:	Profit:

Date:_____ # Inventory Log

Brand:	Type:	Model:	Flaws:
Accessories:		Serial:	
Condition:	Color:	Listed: PM ___ EBY ___ MER___ Other:_____	Function:
Category:	Tested:	Cost:	Sold Price:	Loc:	SKU#
Notes:		Date Acquired:	Sold on:	Profit:

Brand:	Type:	Model:	Flaws:
Accessories:		Serial:	
Condition:	Color:	Listed: PM ___ EBY ___ MER___ Other:_____	Function:
Category:	Tested:	Cost:	Sold Price:	Loc:	SKU#
Notes:		Date Acquired:	Sold on:	Profit:

Brand:	Type:	Model:	Flaws:
Accessories:		Serial:	
Condition:	Color:	Listed: PM ___ EBY ___ MER___ Other:_____	Function:
Category:	Tested:	Cost:	Sold Price:	Loc:	SKU#
Notes:		Date Acquired:	Sold on:	Profit:

Brand:	Type:	Model:	Flaws:
Accessories:		Serial:	
Condition:	Color:	Listed: PM ___ EBY ___ MER___ Other:_____	Function:
Category:	Tested:	Cost:	Sold Price:	Loc:	SKU#
Notes:		Date Acquired:	Sold on:	Profit:

Date:_____ # Inventory Log

Brand:	Type:	Model:	Flaws:
Accessories:		Serial:	
Condition:	Color:	Listed: PM ___ EBY ___ MER___ Other:_____	Function:
Category:	Tested:	Cost:	Sold Price:	Loc: SKU#
Notes:		Date Acquired:	Sold on:	Profit:

Brand:	Type:	Model:	Flaws:
Accessories:		Serial:	
Condition:	Color:	Listed: PM ___ EBY ___ MER___ Other:_____	Function:
Category:	Tested:	Cost:	Sold Price:	Loc: SKU#
Notes:		Date Acquired:	Sold on:	Profit:

Brand:	Type:	Model:	Flaws:
Accessories:		Serial:	
Condition:	Color:	Listed: PM ___ EBY ___ MER___ Other:_____	Function:
Category:	Tested:	Cost:	Sold Price:	Loc: SKU#
Notes:		Date Acquired:	Sold on:	Profit:

Brand:	Type:	Model:	Flaws:
Accessories:		Serial:	
Condition:	Color:	Listed: PM ___ EBY ___ MER___ Other:_____	Function:
Category:	Tested:	Cost:	Sold Price:	Loc: SKU#
Notes:		Date Acquired:	Sold on:	Profit:

Date:_____   # Inventory Log

Brand:	Type:	Model:		Flaws:	
Accessories:		Serial:			
Condition:	Color:	Listed: PM ___ EBY ___ MER___ Other:_____		Function:	
Category:	Tested:	Cost:	Sold Price:	Loc:	SKU#
Notes:		Date Acquired:		Sold on:	Profit:

Brand:	Type:	Model:		Flaws:	
Accessories:		Serial:			
Condition:	Color:	Listed: PM ___ EBY ___ MER___ Other:_____		Function:	
Category:	Tested:	Cost:	Sold Price:	Loc:	SKU#
Notes:		Date Acquired:		Sold on:	Profit:

Brand:	Type:	Model:		Flaws:	
Accessories:		Serial:			
Condition:	Color:	Listed: PM ___ EBY ___ MER___ Other:_____		Function:	
Category:	Tested:	Cost:	Sold Price:	Loc:	SKU#
Notes:		Date Acquired:		Sold on:	Profit:

Brand:	Type:	Model:		Flaws:	
Accessories:		Serial:			
Condition:	Color:	Listed: PM ___ EBY ___ MER___ Other:_____		Function:	
Category:	Tested:	Cost:	Sold Price:	Loc:	SKU#
Notes:		Date Acquired:		Sold on:	Profit:

Date:_____   # Inventory Log

Brand:	Type:	Model:	Flaws:
Accessories:		Serial:	
Condition:	Color:	Listed: PM ___ EBY ___ MER___ Other:_____	Function:
Category:	Tested:	Cost:	Sold Price:	Loc: SKU#
Notes:		Date Acquired:	Sold on:	Profit:

Brand:	Type:	Model:	Flaws:
Accessories:		Serial:	
Condition:	Color:	Listed: PM ___ EBY ___ MER___ Other:_____	Function:
Category:	Tested:	Cost:	Sold Price:	Loc: SKU#
Notes:		Date Acquired:	Sold on:	Profit:

Brand:	Type:	Model:	Flaws:
Accessories:		Serial:	
Condition:	Color:	Listed: PM ___ EBY ___ MER___ Other:_____	Function:
Category:	Tested:	Cost:	Sold Price:	Loc: SKU#
Notes:		Date Acquired:	Sold on:	Profit:

Brand:	Type:	Model:	Flaws:
Accessories:		Serial:	
Condition:	Color:	Listed: PM ___ EBY ___ MER___ Other:_____	Function:
Category:	Tested:	Cost:	Sold Price:	Loc: SKU#
Notes:		Date Acquired:	Sold on:	Profit:

Date:_____ # Inventory Log

Brand:	Type:	Model:		Flaws:	
Accessories:		Serial:			
Condition:	Color:	Listed: PM ___ EBY ___ MER___ Other:_____		Function:	
Category:	Tested:	Cost:	Sold Price:	Loc: SKU#	
Notes:		Date Acquired:		Sold on:	Profit:

Brand:	Type:	Model:		Flaws:	
Accessories:		Serial:			
Condition:	Color:	Listed: PM ___ EBY ___ MER___ Other:_____		Function:	
Category:	Tested:	Cost:	Sold Price:	Loc: SKU#	
Notes:		Date Acquired:		Sold on:	Profit:

Brand:	Type:	Model:		Flaws:	
Accessories:		Serial:			
Condition:	Color:	Listed: PM ___ EBY ___ MER___ Other:_____		Function:	
Category:	Tested:	Cost:	Sold Price:	Loc: SKU#	
Notes:		Date Acquired:		Sold on:	Profit:

Brand:	Type:	Model:		Flaws:	
Accessories:		Serial:			
Condition:	Color:	Listed: PM ___ EBY ___ MER___ Other:_____		Function:	
Category:	Tested:	Cost:	Sold Price:	Loc: SKU#	
Notes:		Date Acquired:		Sold on:	Profit:

Date:_____ # Inventory Log

Brand:	Type:	Model:		Flaws:	
Accessories:		Serial:			
Condition:	Color:	Listed: PM ___ EBY ___ MER___ Other:_____		Function:	
Category:	Tested:	Cost:	Sold Price:	Loc: SKU#	
Notes:		Date Acquired:		Sold on:	Profit:

Brand:	Type:	Model:		Flaws:	
Accessories:		Serial:			
Condition:	Color:	Listed: PM ___ EBY ___ MER___ Other:_____		Function:	
Category:	Tested:	Cost:	Sold Price:	Loc: SKU#	
Notes:		Date Acquired:		Sold on:	Profit:

Brand:	Type:	Model:		Flaws:	
Accessories:		Serial:			
Condition:	Color:	Listed: PM ___ EBY ___ MER___ Other:_____		Function:	
Category:	Tested:	Cost:	Sold Price:	Loc: SKU#	
Notes:		Date Acquired:		Sold on:	Profit:

Brand:	Type:	Model:		Flaws:	
Accessories:		Serial:			
Condition:	Color:	Listed: PM ___ EBY ___ MER___ Other:_____		Function:	
Category:	Tested:	Cost:	Sold Price:	Loc: SKU#	
Notes:		Date Acquired:		Sold on:	Profit:

Date:_____   # Inventory Log

Brand:	Type:	Model:		Flaws:	
Accessories:		Serial:			
Condition:	Color:	Listed: PM ___ EBY ___ MER___ Other:_____		Function:	
Category:	Tested:	Cost:	Sold Price:	Loc: SKU#	
Notes:		Date Acquired:		Sold on:	Profit:

Brand:	Type:	Model:		Flaws:	
Accessories:		Serial:			
Condition:	Color:	Listed: PM ___ EBY ___ MER___ Other:_____		Function:	
Category:	Tested:	Cost:	Sold Price:	Loc: SKU#	
Notes:		Date Acquired:		Sold on:	Profit:

Brand:	Type:	Model:		Flaws:	
Accessories:		Serial:			
Condition:	Color:	Listed: PM ___ EBY ___ MER___ Other:_____		Function:	
Category:	Tested:	Cost:	Sold Price:	Loc: SKU#	
Notes:		Date Acquired:		Sold on:	Profit:

Brand:	Type:	Model:		Flaws:	
Accessories:		Serial:			
Condition:	Color:	Listed: PM ___ EBY ___ MER___ Other:_____		Function:	
Category:	Tested:	Cost:	Sold Price:	Loc: SKU#	
Notes:		Date Acquired:		Sold on:	Profit:

Date:_____ # Inventory Log

Brand:	Type:	Model:	Flaws:
Accessories:		Serial:	
Condition:	Color:	Listed: PM ___ EBY ___ MER___ Other:_____	Function:
Category:	Tested:	Cost:	Sold Price:	Loc: SKU#
Notes:		Date Acquired:	Sold on:	Profit:

Brand:	Type:	Model:	Flaws:
Accessories:		Serial:	
Condition:	Color:	Listed: PM ___ EBY ___ MER___ Other:_____	Function:
Category:	Tested:	Cost:	Sold Price:	Loc: SKU#
Notes:		Date Acquired:	Sold on:	Profit:

Brand:	Type:	Model:	Flaws:
Accessories:		Serial:	
Condition:	Color:	Listed: PM ___ EBY ___ MER___ Other:_____	Function:
Category:	Tested:	Cost:	Sold Price:	Loc: SKU#
Notes:		Date Acquired:	Sold on:	Profit:

Brand:	Type:	Model:	Flaws:
Accessories:		Serial:	
Condition:	Color:	Listed: PM ___ EBY ___ MER___ Other:_____	Function:
Category:	Tested:	Cost:	Sold Price:	Loc: SKU#
Notes:		Date Acquired:	Sold on:	Profit:

Date:_____ # Inventory Log

Brand:	Type:	Model:		Flaws:	
Accessories:		Serial:			
Condition:	Color:	Listed: PM ___ EBY ___ MER___ Other:_____		Function:	
Category:	Tested:	Cost:	Sold Price:	Loc:	SKU#
Notes:		Date Acquired:		Sold on:	Profit:

Brand:	Type:	Model:		Flaws:	
Accessories:		Serial:			
Condition:	Color:	Listed: PM ___ EBY ___ MER___ Other:_____		Function:	
Category:	Tested:	Cost:	Sold Price:	Loc:	SKU#
Notes:		Date Acquired:		Sold on:	Profit:

Brand:	Type:	Model:		Flaws:	
Accessories:		Serial:			
Condition:	Color:	Listed: PM ___ EBY ___ MER___ Other:_____		Function:	
Category:	Tested:	Cost:	Sold Price:	Loc:	SKU#
Notes:		Date Acquired:		Sold on:	Profit:

Brand:	Type:	Model:		Flaws:	
Accessories:		Serial:			
Condition:	Color:	Listed: PM ___ EBY ___ MER___ Other:_____		Function:	
Category:	Tested:	Cost:	Sold Price:	Loc:	SKU#
Notes:		Date Acquired:		Sold on:	Profit:

Date:_____ **Inventory Log**

Brand:	Type:	Model:		Flaws:	
Accessories:		Serial:			
Condition:	Color:	Listed: PM ___ EBY ___ MER___ Other:_____		Function:	
Category:	Tested:	Cost:	Sold Price:	Loc: SKU#	
Notes:		Date Acquired:		Sold on:	Profit:

Brand:	Type:	Model:		Flaws:	
Accessories:		Serial:			
Condition:	Color:	Listed: PM ___ EBY ___ MER___ Other:_____		Function:	
Category:	Tested:	Cost:	Sold Price:	Loc: SKU#	
Notes:		Date Acquired:		Sold on:	Profit:

Brand:	Type:	Model:		Flaws:	
Accessories:		Serial:			
Condition:	Color:	Listed: PM ___ EBY ___ MER___ Other:_____		Function:	
Category:	Tested:	Cost:	Sold Price:	Loc: SKU#	
Notes:		Date Acquired:		Sold on:	Profit:

Brand:	Type:	Model:		Flaws:	
Accessories:		Serial:			
Condition:	Color:	Listed: PM ___ EBY ___ MER___ Other:_____		Function:	
Category:	Tested:	Cost:	Sold Price:	Loc: SKU#	
Notes:		Date Acquired:		Sold on:	Profit:

Inventory Log

Date:_____

Brand:	Type:	Model:		Flaws:	
Accessories:		Serial:			
Condition:	Color:	Listed: PM ___ EBY ___ MER___ Other:_____		Function:	
Category:	Tested:	Cost:	Sold Price:	Loc:	SKU#
Notes:		Date Acquired:		Sold on:	Profit:

Brand:	Type:	Model:		Flaws:	
Accessories:		Serial:			
Condition:	Color:	Listed: PM ___ EBY ___ MER___ Other:_____		Function:	
Category:	Tested:	Cost:	Sold Price:	Loc:	SKU#
Notes:		Date Acquired:		Sold on:	Profit:

Brand:	Type:	Model:		Flaws:	
Accessories:		Serial:			
Condition:	Color:	Listed: PM ___ EBY ___ MER___ Other:_____		Function:	
Category:	Tested:	Cost:	Sold Price:	Loc:	SKU#
Notes:		Date Acquired:		Sold on:	Profit:

Brand:	Type:	Model:		Flaws:	
Accessories:		Serial:			
Condition:	Color:	Listed: PM ___ EBY ___ MER___ Other:_____		Function:	
Category:	Tested:	Cost:	Sold Price:	Loc:	SKU#
Notes:		Date Acquired:		Sold on:	Profit:

Date:_____   # Inventory Log

Brand:	Type:	Model:	Flaws:
Accessories:		Serial:	
Condition:	Color:	Listed: PM ___ EBY ___ MER___ Other:_____	Function:
Category:	Tested:	Cost:	Sold Price:	Loc: SKU#
Notes:		Date Acquired:	Sold on:	Profit:

Brand:	Type:	Model:	Flaws:
Accessories:		Serial:	
Condition:	Color:	Listed: PM ___ EBY ___ MER___ Other:_____	Function:
Category:	Tested:	Cost:	Sold Price:	Loc: SKU#
Notes:		Date Acquired:	Sold on:	Profit:

Brand:	Type:	Model:	Flaws:
Accessories:		Serial:	
Condition:	Color:	Listed: PM ___ EBY ___ MER___ Other:_____	Function:
Category:	Tested:	Cost:	Sold Price:	Loc: SKU#
Notes:		Date Acquired:	Sold on:	Profit:

Brand:	Type:	Model:	Flaws:
Accessories:		Serial:	
Condition:	Color:	Listed: PM ___ EBY ___ MER___ Other:_____	Function:
Category:	Tested:	Cost:	Sold Price:	Loc: SKU#
Notes:		Date Acquired:	Sold on:	Profit:

Date:_____ # Inventory Log

Brand:	Type:	Model:	Flaws:
Accessories:		Serial:	
Condition:	Color:	Listed: PM ___ EBY ___ MER___ Other:_____	Function:
Category:	Tested:	Cost:	Sold Price:	Loc:	SKU#
Notes:		Date Acquired:	Sold on:	Profit:

Brand:	Type:	Model:	Flaws:
Accessories:		Serial:	
Condition:	Color:	Listed: PM ___ EBY ___ MER___ Other:_____	Function:
Category:	Tested:	Cost:	Sold Price:	Loc:	SKU#
Notes:		Date Acquired:	Sold on:	Profit:

Brand:	Type:	Model:	Flaws:
Accessories:		Serial:	
Condition:	Color:	Listed: PM ___ EBY ___ MER___ Other:_____	Function:
Category:	Tested:	Cost:	Sold Price:	Loc:	SKU#
Notes:		Date Acquired:	Sold on:	Profit:

Brand:	Type:	Model:	Flaws:
Accessories:		Serial:	
Condition:	Color:	Listed: PM ___ EBY ___ MER___ Other:_____	Function:
Category:	Tested:	Cost:	Sold Price:	Loc:	SKU#
Notes:		Date Acquired:	Sold on:	Profit:

Date:_____   # Inventory Log

Brand:	Type:	Model:	Flaws:
Accessories:		Serial:	
Condition:	Color:	Listed: PM ___ EBY ___ MER___ Other:_____	Function:
Category:	Tested:	Cost:	Sold Price:	Loc: SKU#
Notes:		Date Acquired:	Sold on:	Profit:

Brand:	Type:	Model:	Flaws:
Accessories:		Serial:	
Condition:	Color:	Listed: PM ___ EBY ___ MER___ Other:_____	Function:
Category:	Tested:	Cost:	Sold Price:	Loc: SKU#
Notes:		Date Acquired:	Sold on:	Profit:

Brand:	Type:	Model:	Flaws:
Accessories:		Serial:	
Condition:	Color:	Listed: PM ___ EBY ___ MER___ Other:_____	Function:
Category:	Tested:	Cost:	Sold Price:	Loc: SKU#
Notes:		Date Acquired:	Sold on:	Profit:

Brand:	Type:	Model:	Flaws:
Accessories:		Serial:	
Condition:	Color:	Listed: PM ___ EBY ___ MER___ Other:_____	Function:
Category:	Tested:	Cost:	Sold Price:	Loc: SKU#
Notes:		Date Acquired:	Sold on:	Profit:

Date:_____

Inventory Log

Brand:	Type:	Model:	Flaws:
Accessories:		Serial:	
Condition:	Color:	Listed: PM ___ EBY ___ MER___ Other:_____	Function:
Category:	Tested:	Cost:	Sold Price:	Loc: SKU#
Notes:		Date Acquired:	Sold on:	Profit:

Brand:	Type:	Model:	Flaws:
Accessories:		Serial:	
Condition:	Color:	Listed: PM ___ EBY ___ MER___ Other:_____	Function:
Category:	Tested:	Cost:	Sold Price:	Loc: SKU#
Notes:		Date Acquired:	Sold on:	Profit:

Brand:	Type:	Model:	Flaws:
Accessories:		Serial:	
Condition:	Color:	Listed: PM ___ EBY ___ MER___ Other:_____	Function:
Category:	Tested:	Cost:	Sold Price:	Loc: SKU#
Notes:		Date Acquired:	Sold on:	Profit:

Brand:	Type:	Model:	Flaws:
Accessories:		Serial:	
Condition:	Color:	Listed: PM ___ EBY ___ MER___ Other:_____	Function:
Category:	Tested:	Cost:	Sold Price:	Loc: SKU#
Notes:		Date Acquired:	Sold on:	Profit:

Date:_____ # Inventory Log

Brand:	Type:	Model:	Flaws:
Accessories:		Serial:	
Condition:	Color:	Listed: PM ___ EBY ___ MER___ Other:_____	Function:
Category:	Tested:	Cost:	Sold Price:	Loc:	SKU#
Notes:		Date Acquired:	Sold on:	Profit:

Brand:	Type:	Model:	Flaws:
Accessories:		Serial:	
Condition:	Color:	Listed: PM ___ EBY ___ MER___ Other:_____	Function:
Category:	Tested:	Cost:	Sold Price:	Loc:	SKU#
Notes:		Date Acquired:	Sold on:	Profit:

Brand:	Type:	Model:	Flaws:
Accessories:		Serial:	
Condition:	Color:	Listed: PM ___ EBY ___ MER___ Other:_____	Function:
Category:	Tested:	Cost:	Sold Price:	Loc:	SKU#
Notes:		Date Acquired:	Sold on:	Profit:

Brand:	Type:	Model:	Flaws:
Accessories:		Serial:	
Condition:	Color:	Listed: PM ___ EBY ___ MER___ Other:_____	Function:
Category:	Tested:	Cost:	Sold Price:	Loc:	SKU#
Notes:		Date Acquired:	Sold on:	Profit:

Date:_____ # Inventory Log

Brand:	Type:	Model:	Flaws:
Accessories:		Serial:	
Condition:	Color:	Listed: PM ___ EBY ___ MER___ Other:_____	Function:
Category:	Tested:	Cost:	Sold Price:	Loc: SKU#
Notes:		Date Acquired:	Sold on:	Profit:

Brand:	Type:	Model:	Flaws:
Accessories:		Serial:	
Condition:	Color:	Listed: PM ___ EBY ___ MER___ Other:_____	Function:
Category:	Tested:	Cost:	Sold Price:	Loc: SKU#
Notes:		Date Acquired:	Sold on:	Profit:

Brand:	Type:	Model:	Flaws:
Accessories:		Serial:	
Condition:	Color:	Listed: PM ___ EBY ___ MER___ Other:_____	Function:
Category:	Tested:	Cost:	Sold Price:	Loc: SKU#
Notes:		Date Acquired:	Sold on:	Profit:

Brand:	Type:	Model:	Flaws:
Accessories:		Serial:	
Condition:	Color:	Listed: PM ___ EBY ___ MER___ Other:_____	Function:
Category:	Tested:	Cost:	Sold Price:	Loc: SKU#
Notes:		Date Acquired:	Sold on:	Profit:

Date:_____ # Inventory Log

Brand:	Type:	Model:	Flaws:
Accessories:		Serial:	
Condition:	Color:	Listed: PM ___ EBY ___ MER___ Other:_____	Function:
Category:	Tested:	Cost:	Sold Price:	Loc: SKU#
Notes:		Date Acquired:	Sold on:	Profit:

Brand:	Type:	Model:	Flaws:
Accessories:		Serial:	
Condition:	Color:	Listed: PM ___ EBY ___ MER___ Other:_____	Function:
Category:	Tested:	Cost:	Sold Price:	Loc: SKU#
Notes:		Date Acquired:	Sold on:	Profit:

Brand:	Type:	Model:	Flaws:
Accessories:		Serial:	
Condition:	Color:	Listed: PM ___ EBY ___ MER___ Other:_____	Function:
Category:	Tested:	Cost:	Sold Price:	Loc: SKU#
Notes:		Date Acquired:	Sold on:	Profit:

Brand:	Type:	Model:	Flaws:
Accessories:		Serial:	
Condition:	Color:	Listed: PM ___ EBY ___ MER___ Other:_____	Function:
Category:	Tested:	Cost:	Sold Price:	Loc: SKU#
Notes:		Date Acquired:	Sold on:	Profit:

Date:_____   # Inventory Log

Brand:	Type:	Model:		Flaws:	
Accessories:		Serial:			
Condition:	Color:	Listed: PM ___ EBY ___ MER___ Other:_____		Function:	
Category:	Tested:	Cost:	Sold Price:	Loc: SKU#	
Notes:		Date Acquired:		Sold on:	Profit:

Brand:	Type:	Model:		Flaws:	
Accessories:		Serial:			
Condition:	Color:	Listed: PM ___ EBY ___ MER___ Other:_____		Function:	
Category:	Tested:	Cost:	Sold Price:	Loc: SKU#	
Notes:		Date Acquired:		Sold on:	Profit:

Brand:	Type:	Model:		Flaws:	
Accessories:		Serial:			
Condition:	Color:	Listed: PM ___ EBY ___ MER___ Other:_____		Function:	
Category:	Tested:	Cost:	Sold Price:	Loc: SKU#	
Notes:		Date Acquired:		Sold on:	Profit:

Brand:	Type:	Model:		Flaws:	
Accessories:		Serial:			
Condition:	Color:	Listed: PM ___ EBY ___ MER___ Other:_____		Function:	
Category:	Tested:	Cost:	Sold Price:	Loc: SKU#	
Notes:		Date Acquired:		Sold on:	Profit:

Date:_____ # Inventory Log

Brand:	Type:	Model:		Flaws:	
Accessories:		Serial:			
Condition:	Color:	Listed: PM ___ EBY ___ MER___ Other:_____		Function:	
Category:	Tested:	Cost:	Sold Price:	Loc: SKU#	
Notes:		Date Acquired:		Sold on:	Profit:

Brand:	Type:	Model:		Flaws:	
Accessories:		Serial:			
Condition:	Color:	Listed: PM ___ EBY ___ MER___ Other:_____		Function:	
Category:	Tested:	Cost:	Sold Price:	Loc: SKU#	
Notes:		Date Acquired:		Sold on:	Profit:

Brand:	Type:	Model:		Flaws:	
Accessories:		Serial:			
Condition:	Color:	Listed: PM ___ EBY ___ MER___ Other:_____		Function:	
Category:	Tested:	Cost:	Sold Price:	Loc: SKU#	
Notes:		Date Acquired:		Sold on:	Profit:

Brand:	Type:	Model:		Flaws:	
Accessories:		Serial:			
Condition:	Color:	Listed: PM ___ EBY ___ MER___ Other:_____		Function:	
Category:	Tested:	Cost:	Sold Price:	Loc: SKU#	
Notes:		Date Acquired:		Sold on:	Profit:

Date:_____   # Inventory Log

Brand:	Type:	Model:	Flaws:
Accessories:		Serial:	
Condition:	Color:	Listed: PM ___ EBY ___ MER___ Other:_____	Function:
Category:	Tested:	Cost:	Sold Price:	Loc: SKU#
Notes:		Date Acquired:	Sold on:	Profit:

Brand:	Type:	Model:	Flaws:
Accessories:		Serial:	
Condition:	Color:	Listed: PM ___ EBY ___ MER___ Other:_____	Function:
Category:	Tested:	Cost:	Sold Price:	Loc: SKU#
Notes:		Date Acquired:	Sold on:	Profit:

Brand:	Type:	Model:	Flaws:
Accessories:		Serial:	
Condition:	Color:	Listed: PM ___ EBY ___ MER___ Other:_____	Function:
Category:	Tested:	Cost:	Sold Price:	Loc: SKU#
Notes:		Date Acquired:	Sold on:	Profit:

Brand:	Type:	Model:	Flaws:
Accessories:		Serial:	
Condition:	Color:	Listed: PM ___ EBY ___ MER___ Other:_____	Function:
Category:	Tested:	Cost:	Sold Price:	Loc: SKU#
Notes:		Date Acquired:	Sold on:	Profit:

Date:_____   # Inventory Log

Brand:	Type:	Model:		Flaws:	
Accessories:		Serial:			
Condition:	Color:	Listed: PM ___ EBY ___ MER___ Other:_____		Function:	
Category:	Tested:	Cost:	Sold Price:	Loc: SKU#	
Notes:		Date Acquired:		Sold on:	Profit:

Brand:	Type:	Model:		Flaws:	
Accessories:		Serial:			
Condition:	Color:	Listed: PM ___ EBY ___ MER___ Other:_____		Function:	
Category:	Tested:	Cost:	Sold Price:	Loc: SKU#	
Notes:		Date Acquired:		Sold on:	Profit:

Brand:	Type:	Model:		Flaws:	
Accessories:		Serial:			
Condition:	Color:	Listed: PM ___ EBY ___ MER___ Other:_____		Function:	
Category:	Tested:	Cost:	Sold Price:	Loc: SKU#	
Notes:		Date Acquired:		Sold on:	Profit:

Brand:	Type:	Model:		Flaws:	
Accessories:		Serial:			
Condition:	Color:	Listed: PM ___ EBY ___ MER___ Other:_____		Function:	
Category:	Tested:	Cost:	Sold Price:	Loc: SKU#	
Notes:		Date Acquired:		Sold on:	Profit:

Date:_____   # Inventory Log

Brand:	Type:	Model:		Flaws:	
Accessories:		Serial:			
Condition:	Color:	Listed: PM ___ EBY ___ MER___ Other:_____		Function:	
Category:	Tested:	Cost:	Sold Price:	Loc: SKU#	
Notes:		Date Acquired:		Sold on:	Profit:

Brand:	Type:	Model:		Flaws:	
Accessories:		Serial:			
Condition:	Color:	Listed: PM ___ EBY ___ MER___ Other:_____		Function:	
Category:	Tested:	Cost:	Sold Price:	Loc: SKU#	
Notes:		Date Acquired:		Sold on:	Profit:

Brand:	Type:	Model:		Flaws:	
Accessories:		Serial:			
Condition:	Color:	Listed: PM ___ EBY ___ MER___ Other:_____		Function:	
Category:	Tested:	Cost:	Sold Price:	Loc: SKU#	
Notes:		Date Acquired:		Sold on:	Profit:

Brand:	Type:	Model:		Flaws:	
Accessories:		Serial:			
Condition:	Color:	Listed: PM ___ EBY ___ MER___ Other:_____		Function:	
Category:	Tested:	Cost:	Sold Price:	Loc: SKU#	
Notes:		Date Acquired:		Sold on:	Profit:

Date:_____   # Inventory Log

Brand:	Type:	Model:		Flaws:	
Accessories:		Serial:			
Condition:	Color:	Listed: PM ___ EBY ___ MER___ Other:_____		Function:	
Category:	Tested:	Cost:	Sold Price:	Loc: SKU#	
Notes:		Date Acquired:		Sold on:	Profit:

Brand:	Type:	Model:		Flaws:	
Accessories:		Serial:			
Condition:	Color:	Listed: PM ___ EBY ___ MER___ Other:_____		Function:	
Category:	Tested:	Cost:	Sold Price:	Loc: SKU#	
Notes:		Date Acquired:		Sold on:	Profit:

Brand:	Type:	Model:		Flaws:	
Accessories:		Serial:			
Condition:	Color:	Listed: PM ___ EBY ___ MER___ Other:_____		Function:	
Category:	Tested:	Cost:	Sold Price:	Loc: SKU#	
Notes:		Date Acquired:		Sold on:	Profit:

Brand:	Type:	Model:		Flaws:	
Accessories:		Serial:			
Condition:	Color:	Listed: PM ___ EBY ___ MER___ Other:_____		Function:	
Category:	Tested:	Cost:	Sold Price:	Loc: SKU#	
Notes:		Date Acquired:		Sold on:	Profit:

Date:_____ # Inventory Log

Brand:	Type:	Model:	Flaws:
Accessories:		Serial:	
Condition:	Color:	Listed: PM ___ EBY ___ MER___ Other:_____	Function:
Category:	Tested:	Cost:	Sold Price:	Loc:	SKU#
Notes:		Date Acquired:	Sold on:	Profit:

Brand:	Type:	Model:	Flaws:
Accessories:		Serial:	
Condition:	Color:	Listed: PM ___ EBY ___ MER___ Other:_____	Function:
Category:	Tested:	Cost:	Sold Price:	Loc:	SKU#
Notes:		Date Acquired:	Sold on:	Profit:

Brand:	Type:	Model:	Flaws:
Accessories:		Serial:	
Condition:	Color:	Listed: PM ___ EBY ___ MER___ Other:_____	Function:
Category:	Tested:	Cost:	Sold Price:	Loc:	SKU#
Notes:		Date Acquired:	Sold on:	Profit:

Brand:	Type:	Model:	Flaws:
Accessories:		Serial:	
Condition:	Color:	Listed: PM ___ EBY ___ MER___ Other:_____	Function:
Category:	Tested:	Cost:	Sold Price:	Loc:	SKU#
Notes:		Date Acquired:	Sold on:	Profit:

Date:_____ # Inventory Log

Brand:	Type:	Model:		Flaws:	
Accessories:		Serial:			
Condition:	Color:	Listed: PM ___ EBY ___ MER___ Other:_____		Function:	
Category:	Tested:	Cost:	Sold Price:	Loc: SKU#	
Notes:		Date Acquired:	Sold on:	Profit:	

Brand:	Type:	Model:		Flaws:	
Accessories:		Serial:			
Condition:	Color:	Listed: PM ___ EBY ___ MER___ Other:_____		Function:	
Category:	Tested:	Cost:	Sold Price:	Loc: SKU#	
Notes:		Date Acquired:	Sold on:	Profit:	

Brand:	Type:	Model:		Flaws:	
Accessories:		Serial:			
Condition:	Color:	Listed: PM ___ EBY ___ MER___ Other:_____		Function:	
Category:	Tested:	Cost:	Sold Price:	Loc: SKU#	
Notes:		Date Acquired:	Sold on:	Profit:	

Brand:	Type:	Model:		Flaws:	
Accessories:		Serial:			
Condition:	Color:	Listed: PM ___ EBY ___ MER___ Other:_____		Function:	
Category:	Tested:	Cost:	Sold Price:	Loc: SKU#	
Notes:		Date Acquired:	Sold on:	Profit:	

Date:_____ # Inventory Log

Brand:	Type:	Model:		Flaws:	
Accessories:		Serial:			
Condition:	Color:	Listed: PM ___ EBY ___ MER___ Other:_____		Function:	
Category:	Tested:	Cost:	Sold Price:	Loc:	SKU#
Notes:		Date Acquired:		Sold on:	Profit:

Brand:	Type:	Model:		Flaws:	
Accessories:		Serial:			
Condition:	Color:	Listed: PM ___ EBY ___ MER___ Other:_____		Function:	
Category:	Tested:	Cost:	Sold Price:	Loc:	SKU#
Notes:		Date Acquired:		Sold on:	Profit:

Brand:	Type:	Model:		Flaws:	
Accessories:		Serial:			
Condition:	Color:	Listed: PM ___ EBY ___ MER___ Other:_____		Function:	
Category:	Tested:	Cost:	Sold Price:	Loc:	SKU#
Notes:		Date Acquired:		Sold on:	Profit:

Brand:	Type:	Model:		Flaws:	
Accessories:		Serial:			
Condition:	Color:	Listed: PM ___ EBY ___ MER___ Other:_____		Function:	
Category:	Tested:	Cost:	Sold Price:	Loc:	SKU#
Notes:		Date Acquired:		Sold on:	Profit:

Date:_____ # Inventory Log

Brand:	Type:	Model:		Flaws:	
Accessories:		Serial:			
Condition:	Color:	Listed: PM ___ EBY ___ MER___ Other:_____		Function:	
Category:	Tested:	Cost:	Sold Price:	Loc:	SKU#
Notes:		Date Acquired:		Sold on:	Profit:

Brand:	Type:	Model:		Flaws:	
Accessories:		Serial:			
Condition:	Color:	Listed: PM ___ EBY ___ MER___ Other:_____		Function:	
Category:	Tested:	Cost:	Sold Price:	Loc:	SKU#
Notes:		Date Acquired:		Sold on:	Profit:

Brand:	Type:	Model:		Flaws:	
Accessories:		Serial:			
Condition:	Color:	Listed: PM ___ EBY ___ MER___ Other:_____		Function:	
Category:	Tested:	Cost:	Sold Price:	Loc:	SKU#
Notes:		Date Acquired:		Sold on:	Profit:

Brand:	Type:	Model:		Flaws:	
Accessories:		Serial:			
Condition:	Color:	Listed: PM ___ EBY ___ MER___ Other:_____		Function:	
Category:	Tested:	Cost:	Sold Price:	Loc:	SKU#
Notes:		Date Acquired:		Sold on:	Profit:

Date:_____ **Inventory Log**

Brand:	Type:	Model:	Flaws:
Accessories:		Serial:	
Condition:	Color:	Listed: PM ___ EBY ___ MER___ Other:_____	Function:
Category:	Tested:	Cost:	Sold Price:	Loc:	SKU#
Notes:		Date Acquired:	Sold on:	Profit:

Brand:	Type:	Model:	Flaws:
Accessories:		Serial:	
Condition:	Color:	Listed: PM ___ EBY ___ MER___ Other:_____	Function:
Category:	Tested:	Cost:	Sold Price:	Loc:	SKU#
Notes:		Date Acquired:	Sold on:	Profit:

Brand:	Type:	Model:	Flaws:
Accessories:		Serial:	
Condition:	Color:	Listed: PM ___ EBY ___ MER___ Other:_____	Function:
Category:	Tested:	Cost:	Sold Price:	Loc:	SKU#
Notes:		Date Acquired:	Sold on:	Profit:

Brand:	Type:	Model:	Flaws:
Accessories:		Serial:	
Condition:	Color:	Listed: PM ___ EBY ___ MER___ Other:_____	Function:
Category:	Tested:	Cost:	Sold Price:	Loc:	SKU#
Notes:		Date Acquired:	Sold on:	Profit:

Date:_____   # Inventory Log

Brand:	Type:	Model:	Flaws:
Accessories:		Serial:	
Condition:	Color:	Listed: PM ___ EBY ___ MER___ Other:_____	Function:
Category:	Tested:	Cost:	Sold Price:	Loc: SKU#
Notes:		Date Acquired:	Sold on:	Profit:

Brand:	Type:	Model:	Flaws:
Accessories:		Serial:	
Condition:	Color:	Listed: PM ___ EBY ___ MER___ Other:_____	Function:
Category:	Tested:	Cost:	Sold Price:	Loc: SKU#
Notes:		Date Acquired:	Sold on:	Profit:

Brand:	Type:	Model:	Flaws:
Accessories:		Serial:	
Condition:	Color:	Listed: PM ___ EBY ___ MER___ Other:_____	Function:
Category:	Tested:	Cost:	Sold Price:	Loc: SKU#
Notes:		Date Acquired:	Sold on:	Profit:

Brand:	Type:	Model:	Flaws:
Accessories:		Serial:	
Condition:	Color:	Listed: PM ___ EBY ___ MER___ Other:_____	Function:
Category:	Tested:	Cost:	Sold Price:	Loc: SKU#
Notes:		Date Acquired:	Sold on:	Profit:

Date:_____   # Inventory Log

Brand:	Type:	Model:		Flaws:	
Accessories:		Serial:			
Condition:	Color:	Listed: PM ___ EBY ___ MER ___ Other:_____		Function:	
Category:	Tested:	Cost:	Sold Price:	Loc: SKU#	
Notes:		Date Acquired:		Sold on:	Profit:

Brand:	Type:	Model:		Flaws:	
Accessories:		Serial:			
Condition:	Color:	Listed: PM ___ EBY ___ MER ___ Other:_____		Function:	
Category:	Tested:	Cost:	Sold Price:	Loc: SKU#	
Notes:		Date Acquired:		Sold on:	Profit:

Brand:	Type:	Model:		Flaws:	
Accessories:		Serial:			
Condition:	Color:	Listed: PM ___ EBY ___ MER ___ Other:_____		Function:	
Category:	Tested:	Cost:	Sold Price:	Loc: SKU#	
Notes:		Date Acquired:		Sold on:	Profit:

Brand:	Type:	Model:		Flaws:	
Accessories:		Serial:			
Condition:	Color:	Listed: PM ___ EBY ___ MER ___ Other:_____		Function:	
Category:	Tested:	Cost:	Sold Price:	Loc: SKU#	
Notes:		Date Acquired:		Sold on:	Profit:

Date:_____ # Inventory Log

Brand:	Type:	Model:	Flaws:
Accessories:		Serial:	
Condition:	Color:	Listed: PM ___ EBY ___ MER___ Other:_____	Function:
Category:	Tested:	Cost:	Sold Price:	Loc: SKU#
Notes:		Date Acquired:	Sold on:	Profit:

Brand:	Type:	Model:	Flaws:
Accessories:		Serial:	
Condition:	Color:	Listed: PM ___ EBY ___ MER___ Other:_____	Function:
Category:	Tested:	Cost:	Sold Price:	Loc: SKU#
Notes:		Date Acquired:	Sold on:	Profit:

Brand:	Type:	Model:	Flaws:
Accessories:		Serial:	
Condition:	Color:	Listed: PM ___ EBY ___ MER___ Other:_____	Function:
Category:	Tested:	Cost:	Sold Price:	Loc: SKU#
Notes:		Date Acquired:	Sold on:	Profit:

Brand:	Type:	Model:	Flaws:
Accessories:		Serial:	
Condition:	Color:	Listed: PM ___ EBY ___ MER___ Other:_____	Function:
Category:	Tested:	Cost:	Sold Price:	Loc: SKU#
Notes:		Date Acquired:	Sold on:	Profit:

Date:_____ # Inventory Log

Brand:	Type:	Model:		Flaws:	
Accessories:		Serial:			
Condition:	Color:	Listed: PM ___ EBY ___ MER___ Other:_____		Function:	
Category:	Tested:	Cost:	Sold Price:	Loc: SKU#	
Notes:		Date Acquired:		Sold on:	Profit:

Brand:	Type:	Model:		Flaws:	
Accessories:		Serial:			
Condition:	Color:	Listed: PM ___ EBY ___ MER___ Other:_____		Function:	
Category:	Tested:	Cost:	Sold Price:	Loc: SKU#	
Notes:		Date Acquired:		Sold on:	Profit:

Brand:	Type:	Model:		Flaws:	
Accessories:		Serial:			
Condition:	Color:	Listed: PM ___ EBY ___ MER___ Other:_____		Function:	
Category:	Tested:	Cost:	Sold Price:	Loc: SKU#	
Notes:		Date Acquired:		Sold on:	Profit:

Brand:	Type:	Model:		Flaws:	
Accessories:		Serial:			
Condition:	Color:	Listed: PM ___ EBY ___ MER___ Other:_____		Function:	
Category:	Tested:	Cost:	Sold Price:	Loc: SKU#	
Notes:		Date Acquired:		Sold on:	Profit:

Date:_____ # Inventory Log

Brand:	Type:	Model:	Flaws:
Accessories:		Serial:	
Condition:	Color:	Listed: PM ___ EBY ___ MER___ Other:_____	Function:
Category:	Tested:	Cost:	Sold Price:	Loc:	SKU#
Notes:		Date Acquired:	Sold on:	Profit:

Brand:	Type:	Model:	Flaws:
Accessories:		Serial:	
Condition:	Color:	Listed: PM ___ EBY ___ MER___ Other:_____	Function:
Category:	Tested:	Cost:	Sold Price:	Loc:	SKU#
Notes:		Date Acquired:	Sold on:	Profit:

Brand:	Type:	Model:	Flaws:
Accessories:		Serial:	
Condition:	Color:	Listed: PM ___ EBY ___ MER___ Other:_____	Function:
Category:	Tested:	Cost:	Sold Price:	Loc:	SKU#
Notes:		Date Acquired:	Sold on:	Profit:

Brand:	Type:	Model:	Flaws:
Accessories:		Serial:	
Condition:	Color:	Listed: PM ___ EBY ___ MER___ Other:_____	Function:
Category:	Tested:	Cost:	Sold Price:	Loc:	SKU#
Notes:		Date Acquired:	Sold on:	Profit:

Date:_____ # Inventory Log

Brand:	Type:	Model:		Flaws:	
Accessories:		Serial:			
Condition:	Color:	Listed: PM ___ EBY ___ MER___ Other:_____		Function:	
Category:	Tested:	Cost:	Sold Price:	Loc: SKU#	
Notes:		Date Acquired:		Sold on:	Profit:

Brand:	Type:	Model:		Flaws:	
Accessories:		Serial:			
Condition:	Color:	Listed: PM ___ EBY ___ MER___ Other:_____		Function:	
Category:	Tested:	Cost:	Sold Price:	Loc: SKU#	
Notes:		Date Acquired:		Sold on:	Profit:

Brand:	Type:	Model:		Flaws:	
Accessories:		Serial:			
Condition:	Color:	Listed: PM ___ EBY ___ MER___ Other:_____		Function:	
Category:	Tested:	Cost:	Sold Price:	Loc: SKU#	
Notes:		Date Acquired:		Sold on:	Profit:

Brand:	Type:	Model:		Flaws:	
Accessories:		Serial:			
Condition:	Color:	Listed: PM ___ EBY ___ MER___ Other:_____		Function:	
Category:	Tested:	Cost:	Sold Price:	Loc: SKU#	
Notes:		Date Acquired:		Sold on:	Profit:

Date:_____ # Inventory Log

Brand:	Type:	Model:		Flaws:	
Accessories:		Serial:			
Condition:	Color:	Listed: PM ___ EBY ___ MER___ Other:_____		Function:	
Category:	Tested:	Cost:	Sold Price:	Loc:	SKU#
Notes:		Date Acquired:		Sold on:	Profit:

Brand:	Type:	Model:		Flaws:	
Accessories:		Serial:			
Condition:	Color:	Listed: PM ___ EBY ___ MER___ Other:_____		Function:	
Category:	Tested:	Cost:	Sold Price:	Loc:	SKU#
Notes:		Date Acquired:		Sold on:	Profit:

Brand:	Type:	Model:		Flaws:	
Accessories:		Serial:			
Condition:	Color:	Listed: PM ___ EBY ___ MER___ Other:_____		Function:	
Category:	Tested:	Cost:	Sold Price:	Loc:	SKU#
Notes:		Date Acquired:		Sold on:	Profit:

Brand:	Type:	Model:		Flaws:	
Accessories:		Serial:			
Condition:	Color:	Listed: PM ___ EBY ___ MER___ Other:_____		Function:	
Category:	Tested:	Cost:	Sold Price:	Loc:	SKU#
Notes:		Date Acquired:		Sold on:	Profit:

Date:_____ # Inventory Log

Brand:	Type:	Model:		Flaws:	
Accessories:		Serial:			
Condition:	Color:	Listed: PM ___ EBY ___ MER___ Other:_____		Function:	
Category:	Tested:	Cost:	Sold Price:	Loc:	SKU#
Notes:		Date Acquired:		Sold on:	Profit:

Brand:	Type:	Model:		Flaws:	
Accessories:		Serial:			
Condition:	Color:	Listed: PM ___ EBY ___ MER___ Other:_____		Function:	
Category:	Tested:	Cost:	Sold Price:	Loc:	SKU#
Notes:		Date Acquired:		Sold on:	Profit:

Brand:	Type:	Model:		Flaws:	
Accessories:		Serial:			
Condition:	Color:	Listed: PM ___ EBY ___ MER___ Other:_____		Function:	
Category:	Tested:	Cost:	Sold Price:	Loc:	SKU#
Notes:		Date Acquired:		Sold on:	Profit:

Brand:	Type:	Model:		Flaws:	
Accessories:		Serial:			
Condition:	Color:	Listed: PM ___ EBY ___ MER___ Other:_____		Function:	
Category:	Tested:	Cost:	Sold Price:	Loc:	SKU#
Notes:		Date Acquired:		Sold on:	Profit:

Date:_____   # Inventory Log

Brand:	Type:	Model:		Flaws:	
Accessories:		Serial:			
Condition:	Color:	Listed: PM ___ EBY ___ MER___ Other:_____		Function:	
Category:	Tested:	Cost:	Sold Price:	Loc: SKU#	
Notes:		Date Acquired:		Sold on:	Profit:

Brand:	Type:	Model:		Flaws:	
Accessories:		Serial:			
Condition:	Color:	Listed: PM ___ EBY ___ MER___ Other:_____		Function:	
Category:	Tested:	Cost:	Sold Price:	Loc: SKU#	
Notes:		Date Acquired:		Sold on:	Profit:

Brand:	Type:	Model:		Flaws:	
Accessories:		Serial:			
Condition:	Color:	Listed: PM ___ EBY ___ MER___ Other:_____		Function:	
Category:	Tested:	Cost:	Sold Price:	Loc: SKU#	
Notes:		Date Acquired:		Sold on:	Profit:

Brand:	Type:	Model:		Flaws:	
Accessories:		Serial:			
Condition:	Color:	Listed: PM ___ EBY ___ MER___ Other:_____		Function:	
Category:	Tested:	Cost:	Sold Price:	Loc: SKU#	
Notes:		Date Acquired:		Sold on:	Profit:

Date:_____ # Inventory Log

Brand:	Type:	Model:	Flaws:
Accessories:		Serial:	
Condition:	Color:	Listed: PM ___ EBY ___ MER___ Other:_____	Function:
Category:	Tested:	Cost:	Sold Price:	Loc: SKU#
Notes:		Date Acquired:	Sold on:	Profit:

Brand:	Type:	Model:	Flaws:
Accessories:		Serial:	
Condition:	Color:	Listed: PM ___ EBY ___ MER___ Other:_____	Function:
Category:	Tested:	Cost:	Sold Price:	Loc: SKU#
Notes:		Date Acquired:	Sold on:	Profit:

Brand:	Type:	Model:	Flaws:
Accessories:		Serial:	
Condition:	Color:	Listed: PM ___ EBY ___ MER___ Other:_____	Function:
Category:	Tested:	Cost:	Sold Price:	Loc: SKU#
Notes:		Date Acquired:	Sold on:	Profit:

Brand:	Type:	Model:	Flaws:
Accessories:		Serial:	
Condition:	Color:	Listed: PM ___ EBY ___ MER___ Other:_____	Function:
Category:	Tested:	Cost:	Sold Price:	Loc: SKU#
Notes:		Date Acquired:	Sold on:	Profit:

Date:_____ # Inventory Log

Brand:	Type:	Model:		Flaws:	
Accessories:		Serial:			
Condition:	Color:	Listed: PM ___ EBY ___ MER___ Other:_____		Function:	
Category:	Tested:	Cost:	Sold Price:	Loc:	SKU#
Notes:		Date Acquired:		Sold on:	Profit:

Brand:	Type:	Model:		Flaws:	
Accessories:		Serial:			
Condition:	Color:	Listed: PM ___ EBY ___ MER___ Other:_____		Function:	
Category:	Tested:	Cost:	Sold Price:	Loc:	SKU#
Notes:		Date Acquired:		Sold on:	Profit:

Brand:	Type:	Model:		Flaws:	
Accessories:		Serial:			
Condition:	Color:	Listed: PM ___ EBY ___ MER___ Other:_____		Function:	
Category:	Tested:	Cost:	Sold Price:	Loc:	SKU#
Notes:		Date Acquired:		Sold on:	Profit:

Brand:	Type:	Model:		Flaws:	
Accessories:		Serial:			
Condition:	Color:	Listed: PM ___ EBY ___ MER___ Other:_____		Function:	
Category:	Tested:	Cost:	Sold Price:	Loc:	SKU#
Notes:		Date Acquired:		Sold on:	Profit:

Date:_____ # Inventory Log

Brand:	Type:	Model:	Flaws:
Accessories:		Serial:	
Condition:	Color:	Listed: PM ___ EBY ___ MER___ Other:_____	Function:
Category:	Tested:	Cost:	Sold Price:	Loc: SKU#
Notes:		Date Acquired:	Sold on:	Profit:

Brand:	Type:	Model:	Flaws:
Accessories:		Serial:	
Condition:	Color:	Listed: PM ___ EBY ___ MER___ Other:_____	Function:
Category:	Tested:	Cost:	Sold Price:	Loc: SKU#
Notes:		Date Acquired:	Sold on:	Profit:

Brand:	Type:	Model:	Flaws:
Accessories:		Serial:	
Condition:	Color:	Listed: PM ___ EBY ___ MER___ Other:_____	Function:
Category:	Tested:	Cost:	Sold Price:	Loc: SKU#
Notes:		Date Acquired:	Sold on:	Profit:

Brand:	Type:	Model:	Flaws:
Accessories:		Serial:	
Condition:	Color:	Listed: PM ___ EBY ___ MER___ Other:_____	Function:
Category:	Tested:	Cost:	Sold Price:	Loc: SKU#
Notes:		Date Acquired:	Sold on:	Profit:

Date:_____   # Inventory Log

Brand:	Type:	Model:	Flaws:
Accessories:		Serial:	
Condition:	Color:	Listed: PM ___ EBY ___ MER___ Other:_____	Function:
Category:	Tested:	Cost:	Sold Price:	Loc: SKU#
Notes:		Date Acquired:	Sold on:	Profit:

Brand:	Type:	Model:	Flaws:
Accessories:		Serial:	
Condition:	Color:	Listed: PM ___ EBY ___ MER___ Other:_____	Function:
Category:	Tested:	Cost:	Sold Price:	Loc: SKU#
Notes:		Date Acquired:	Sold on:	Profit:

Brand:	Type:	Model:	Flaws:
Accessories:		Serial:	
Condition:	Color:	Listed: PM ___ EBY ___ MER___ Other:_____	Function:
Category:	Tested:	Cost:	Sold Price:	Loc: SKU#
Notes:		Date Acquired:	Sold on:	Profit:

Brand:	Type:	Model:	Flaws:
Accessories:		Serial:	
Condition:	Color:	Listed: PM ___ EBY ___ MER___ Other:_____	Function:
Category:	Tested:	Cost:	Sold Price:	Loc: SKU#
Notes:		Date Acquired:	Sold on:	Profit:

Date:_____   # Inventory Log

Brand:	Type:	Model:	Flaws:
Accessories:		Serial:	
Condition:	Color:	Listed: PM ___ EBY ___ MER___ Other:_____	Function:
Category:	Tested:	Cost:	Sold Price:	Loc: SKU#
Notes:		Date Acquired:	Sold on:	Profit:

Brand:	Type:	Model:	Flaws:
Accessories:		Serial:	
Condition:	Color:	Listed: PM ___ EBY ___ MER___ Other:_____	Function:
Category:	Tested:	Cost:	Sold Price:	Loc: SKU#
Notes:		Date Acquired:	Sold on:	Profit:

Brand:	Type:	Model:	Flaws:
Accessories:		Serial:	
Condition:	Color:	Listed: PM ___ EBY ___ MER___ Other:_____	Function:
Category:	Tested:	Cost:	Sold Price:	Loc: SKU#
Notes:		Date Acquired:	Sold on:	Profit:

Brand:	Type:	Model:	Flaws:
Accessories:		Serial:	
Condition:	Color:	Listed: PM ___ EBY ___ MER___ Other:_____	Function:
Category:	Tested:	Cost:	Sold Price:	Loc: SKU#
Notes:		Date Acquired:	Sold on:	Profit:

Date:_____   # Inventory Log

Brand:	Type:	Model:	Flaws:
Accessories:		Serial:	
Condition:	Color:	Listed: PM ___ EBY ___ MER___ Other:_____	Function:
Category:	Tested:	Cost:	Sold Price:	Loc: SKU#
Notes:		Date Acquired:	Sold on:	Profit:

Brand:	Type:	Model:	Flaws:
Accessories:		Serial:	
Condition:	Color:	Listed: PM ___ EBY ___ MER___ Other:_____	Function:
Category:	Tested:	Cost:	Sold Price:	Loc: SKU#
Notes:		Date Acquired:	Sold on:	Profit:

Brand:	Type:	Model:	Flaws:
Accessories:		Serial:	
Condition:	Color:	Listed: PM ___ EBY ___ MER___ Other:_____	Function:
Category:	Tested:	Cost:	Sold Price:	Loc: SKU#
Notes:		Date Acquired:	Sold on:	Profit:

Brand:	Type:	Model:	Flaws:
Accessories:		Serial:	
Condition:	Color:	Listed: PM ___ EBY ___ MER___ Other:_____	Function:
Category:	Tested:	Cost:	Sold Price:	Loc: SKU#
Notes:		Date Acquired:	Sold on:	Profit:

Date:_____ # Inventory Log

Brand:	Type:	Model:	Flaws:
Accessories:		Serial:	
Condition:	Color:	Listed: PM ___ EBY ___ MER___ Other:_____	Function:
Category:	Tested:	Cost:	Sold Price:	Loc: SKU#
Notes:		Date Acquired:	Sold on:	Profit:

Brand:	Type:	Model:	Flaws:
Accessories:		Serial:	
Condition:	Color:	Listed: PM ___ EBY ___ MER___ Other:_____	Function:
Category:	Tested:	Cost:	Sold Price:	Loc: SKU#
Notes:		Date Acquired:	Sold on:	Profit:

Brand:	Type:	Model:	Flaws:
Accessories:		Serial:	
Condition:	Color:	Listed: PM ___ EBY ___ MER___ Other:_____	Function:
Category:	Tested:	Cost:	Sold Price:	Loc: SKU#
Notes:		Date Acquired:	Sold on:	Profit:

Brand:	Type:	Model:	Flaws:
Accessories:		Serial:	
Condition:	Color:	Listed: PM ___ EBY ___ MER___ Other:_____	Function:
Category:	Tested:	Cost:	Sold Price:	Loc: SKU#
Notes:		Date Acquired:	Sold on:	Profit:

Date:_____   # Inventory Log

Brand:	Type:	Model:	Flaws:
Accessories:		Serial:	
Condition:	Color:	Listed: PM ___ EBY ___ MER___ Other:_____	Function:
Category:	Tested:	Cost:	Sold Price:	Loc: SKU#
Notes:		Date Acquired:	Sold on:	Profit:

Brand:	Type:	Model:	Flaws:
Accessories:		Serial:	
Condition:	Color:	Listed: PM ___ EBY ___ MER___ Other:_____	Function:
Category:	Tested:	Cost:	Sold Price:	Loc: SKU#
Notes:		Date Acquired:	Sold on:	Profit:

Brand:	Type:	Model:	Flaws:
Accessories:		Serial:	
Condition:	Color:	Listed: PM ___ EBY ___ MER___ Other:_____	Function:
Category:	Tested:	Cost:	Sold Price:	Loc: SKU#
Notes:		Date Acquired:	Sold on:	Profit:

Brand:	Type:	Model:	Flaws:
Accessories:		Serial:	
Condition:	Color:	Listed: PM ___ EBY ___ MER___ Other:_____	Function:
Category:	Tested:	Cost:	Sold Price:	Loc: SKU#
Notes:		Date Acquired:	Sold on:	Profit:

Date:_____   # Inventory Log

Brand:	Type:	Model:	Flaws:
Accessories:		Serial:	
Condition:	Color:	Listed: PM ___ EBY ___ MER___ Other:_____	Function:
Category:	Tested:	Cost:	Sold Price:	Loc: SKU#
Notes:		Date Acquired:	Sold on:	Profit:

Brand:	Type:	Model:	Flaws:
Accessories:		Serial:	
Condition:	Color:	Listed: PM ___ EBY ___ MER___ Other:_____	Function:
Category:	Tested:	Cost:	Sold Price:	Loc: SKU#
Notes:		Date Acquired:	Sold on:	Profit:

Brand:	Type:	Model:	Flaws:
Accessories:		Serial:	
Condition:	Color:	Listed: PM ___ EBY ___ MER___ Other:_____	Function:
Category:	Tested:	Cost:	Sold Price:	Loc: SKU#
Notes:		Date Acquired:	Sold on:	Profit:

Brand:	Type:	Model:	Flaws:
Accessories:		Serial:	
Condition:	Color:	Listed: PM ___ EBY ___ MER___ Other:_____	Function:
Category:	Tested:	Cost:	Sold Price:	Loc: SKU#
Notes:		Date Acquired:	Sold on:	Profit:

Date:_____

Inventory Log

Brand:	Type:	Model:	Flaws:
Accessories:		Serial:	
Condition:	Color:	Listed: PM ___ EBY ___ MER___ Other:_____	Function:
Category:	Tested:	Cost:	Sold Price:	Loc: SKU#
Notes:		Date Acquired:	Sold on:	Profit:

Brand:	Type:	Model:	Flaws:
Accessories:		Serial:	
Condition:	Color:	Listed: PM ___ EBY ___ MER___ Other:_____	Function:
Category:	Tested:	Cost:	Sold Price:	Loc: SKU#
Notes:		Date Acquired:	Sold on:	Profit:

Brand:	Type:	Model:	Flaws:
Accessories:		Serial:	
Condition:	Color:	Listed: PM ___ EBY ___ MER___ Other:_____	Function:
Category:	Tested:	Cost:	Sold Price:	Loc: SKU#
Notes:		Date Acquired:	Sold on:	Profit:

Brand:	Type:	Model:	Flaws:
Accessories:		Serial:	
Condition:	Color:	Listed: PM ___ EBY ___ MER___ Other:_____	Function:
Category:	Tested:	Cost:	Sold Price:	Loc: SKU#
Notes:		Date Acquired:	Sold on:	Profit:

Date:_____   # Inventory Log

Brand:	Type:	Model:	Flaws:
Accessories:		Serial:	
Condition:	Color:	Listed: PM ___ EBY ___ MER___ Other:_____	Function:
Category:	Tested:	Cost:	Sold Price:	Loc:	SKU#
Notes:		Date Acquired:	Sold on:	Profit:

Brand:	Type:	Model:	Flaws:
Accessories:		Serial:	
Condition:	Color:	Listed: PM ___ EBY ___ MER___ Other:_____	Function:
Category:	Tested:	Cost:	Sold Price:	Loc:	SKU#
Notes:		Date Acquired:	Sold on:	Profit:

Brand:	Type:	Model:	Flaws:
Accessories:		Serial:	
Condition:	Color:	Listed: PM ___ EBY ___ MER___ Other:_____	Function:
Category:	Tested:	Cost:	Sold Price:	Loc:	SKU#
Notes:		Date Acquired:	Sold on:	Profit:

Brand:	Type:	Model:	Flaws:
Accessories:		Serial:	
Condition:	Color:	Listed: PM ___ EBY ___ MER___ Other:_____	Function:
Category:	Tested:	Cost:	Sold Price:	Loc:	SKU#
Notes:		Date Acquired:	Sold on:	Profit:

Date:_____   # Inventory Log

Brand:	Type:	Model:	Flaws:
Accessories:		Serial:	
Condition:	Color:	Listed: PM ___ EBY ___ MER___ Other:_____	Function:
Category:	Tested:	Cost:	Sold Price:	Loc: SKU#
Notes:		Date Acquired:	Sold on:	Profit:

Brand:	Type:	Model:	Flaws:
Accessories:		Serial:	
Condition:	Color:	Listed: PM ___ EBY ___ MER___ Other:_____	Function:
Category:	Tested:	Cost:	Sold Price:	Loc: SKU#
Notes:		Date Acquired:	Sold on:	Profit:

Brand:	Type:	Model:	Flaws:
Accessories:		Serial:	
Condition:	Color:	Listed: PM ___ EBY ___ MER___ Other:_____	Function:
Category:	Tested:	Cost:	Sold Price:	Loc: SKU#
Notes:		Date Acquired:	Sold on:	Profit:

Brand:	Type:	Model:	Flaws:
Accessories:		Serial:	
Condition:	Color:	Listed: PM ___ EBY ___ MER___ Other:_____	Function:
Category:	Tested:	Cost:	Sold Price:	Loc: SKU#
Notes:		Date Acquired:	Sold on:	Profit:

Date:_____   # Inventory Log

Brand:	Type:	Model:	Flaws:
Accessories:		Serial:	
Condition:	Color:	Listed: PM ___ EBY ___ MER___ Other:_____	Function:
Category:	Tested:	Cost:	Sold Price:	Loc: SKU#
Notes:		Date Acquired:	Sold on:	Profit:

Brand:	Type:	Model:	Flaws:
Accessories:		Serial:	
Condition:	Color:	Listed: PM ___ EBY ___ MER___ Other:_____	Function:
Category:	Tested:	Cost:	Sold Price:	Loc: SKU#
Notes:		Date Acquired:	Sold on:	Profit:

Brand:	Type:	Model:	Flaws:
Accessories:		Serial:	
Condition:	Color:	Listed: PM ___ EBY ___ MER___ Other:_____	Function:
Category:	Tested:	Cost:	Sold Price:	Loc: SKU#
Notes:		Date Acquired:	Sold on:	Profit:

Brand:	Type:	Model:	Flaws:
Accessories:		Serial:	
Condition:	Color:	Listed: PM ___ EBY ___ MER___ Other:_____	Function:
Category:	Tested:	Cost:	Sold Price:	Loc: SKU#
Notes:		Date Acquired:	Sold on:	Profit:

Date:_____   # Inventory Log

Brand:	Type:	Model:	Flaws:
Accessories:		Serial:	
Condition:	Color:	Listed: PM ___ EBY ___ MER___ Other:_____	Function:
Category:	Tested:	Cost:	Sold Price:	Loc: SKU#
Notes:		Date Acquired:	Sold on:	Profit:

Brand:	Type:	Model:	Flaws:
Accessories:		Serial:	
Condition:	Color:	Listed: PM ___ EBY ___ MER___ Other:_____	Function:
Category:	Tested:	Cost:	Sold Price:	Loc: SKU#
Notes:		Date Acquired:	Sold on:	Profit:

Brand:	Type:	Model:	Flaws:
Accessories:		Serial:	
Condition:	Color:	Listed: PM ___ EBY ___ MER___ Other:_____	Function:
Category:	Tested:	Cost:	Sold Price:	Loc: SKU#
Notes:		Date Acquired:	Sold on:	Profit:

Brand:	Type:	Model:	Flaws:
Accessories:		Serial:	
Condition:	Color:	Listed: PM ___ EBY ___ MER___ Other:_____	Function:
Category:	Tested:	Cost:	Sold Price:	Loc: SKU#
Notes:		Date Acquired:	Sold on:	Profit:

Date:_____   # Inventory Log

Brand:	Type:	Model:	Flaws:
Accessories:		Serial:	
Condition:	Color:	Listed: PM ___ EBY ___ MER___ Other:_____	Function:
Category:	Tested:	Cost: Sold Price:	Loc: SKU#
Notes:		Date Acquired:	Sold on: Profit:

Brand:	Type:	Model:	Flaws:
Accessories:		Serial:	
Condition:	Color:	Listed: PM ___ EBY ___ MER___ Other:_____	Function:
Category:	Tested:	Cost: Sold Price:	Loc: SKU#
Notes:		Date Acquired:	Sold on: Profit:

Brand:	Type:	Model:	Flaws:
Accessories:		Serial:	
Condition:	Color:	Listed: PM ___ EBY ___ MER___ Other:_____	Function:
Category:	Tested:	Cost: Sold Price:	Loc: SKU#
Notes:		Date Acquired:	Sold on: Profit:

Brand:	Type:	Model:	Flaws:
Accessories:		Serial:	
Condition:	Color:	Listed: PM ___ EBY ___ MER___ Other:_____	Function:
Category:	Tested:	Cost: Sold Price:	Loc: SKU#
Notes:		Date Acquired:	Sold on: Profit:

Date:_____   # Inventory Log

Brand:	Type:	Model:		Flaws:	
Accessories:		Serial:			
Condition:	Color:	Listed: PM ___ EBY ___ MER___ Other:_____		Function:	
Category:	Tested:	Cost:	Sold Price:	Loc: SKU#	
Notes:		Date Acquired:		Sold on:	Profit:

Brand:	Type:	Model:		Flaws:	
Accessories:		Serial:			
Condition:	Color:	Listed: PM ___ EBY ___ MER___ Other:_____		Function:	
Category:	Tested:	Cost:	Sold Price:	Loc: SKU#	
Notes:		Date Acquired:		Sold on:	Profit:

Brand:	Type:	Model:		Flaws:	
Accessories:		Serial:			
Condition:	Color:	Listed: PM ___ EBY ___ MER___ Other:_____		Function:	
Category:	Tested:	Cost:	Sold Price:	Loc: SKU#	
Notes:		Date Acquired:		Sold on:	Profit:

Brand:	Type:	Model:		Flaws:	
Accessories:		Serial:			
Condition:	Color:	Listed: PM ___ EBY ___ MER___ Other:_____		Function:	
Category:	Tested:	Cost:	Sold Price:	Loc: SKU#	
Notes:		Date Acquired:		Sold on:	Profit:

Date:_____ # Inventory Log

Brand:	Type:	Model:	Flaws:
Accessories:		Serial:	
Condition:	Color:	Listed: PM ___ EBY ___ MER___ Other:_____	Function:
Category:	Tested:	Cost:	Sold Price:	Loc: SKU#
Notes:		Date Acquired:	Sold on:	Profit:

Brand:	Type:	Model:	Flaws:
Accessories:		Serial:	
Condition:	Color:	Listed: PM ___ EBY ___ MER___ Other:_____	Function:
Category:	Tested:	Cost:	Sold Price:	Loc: SKU#
Notes:		Date Acquired:	Sold on:	Profit:

Brand:	Type:	Model:	Flaws:
Accessories:		Serial:	
Condition:	Color:	Listed: PM ___ EBY ___ MER___ Other:_____	Function:
Category:	Tested:	Cost:	Sold Price:	Loc: SKU#
Notes:		Date Acquired:	Sold on:	Profit:

Brand:	Type:	Model:	Flaws:
Accessories:		Serial:	
Condition:	Color:	Listed: PM ___ EBY ___ MER___ Other:_____	Function:
Category:	Tested:	Cost:	Sold Price:	Loc: SKU#
Notes:		Date Acquired:	Sold on:	Profit:

Date:_____ # Inventory Log

Brand:	Type:	Model:	Flaws:
Accessories:		Serial:	
Condition:	Color:	Listed: PM ___ EBY ___ MER___ Other:_____	Function:
Category:	Tested:	Cost:	Sold Price:	Loc:	SKU#
Notes:		Date Acquired:	Sold on:	Profit:

Brand:	Type:	Model:	Flaws:
Accessories:		Serial:	
Condition:	Color:	Listed: PM ___ EBY ___ MER___ Other:_____	Function:
Category:	Tested:	Cost:	Sold Price:	Loc:	SKU#
Notes:		Date Acquired:	Sold on:	Profit:

Brand:	Type:	Model:	Flaws:
Accessories:		Serial:	
Condition:	Color:	Listed: PM ___ EBY ___ MER___ Other:_____	Function:
Category:	Tested:	Cost:	Sold Price:	Loc:	SKU#
Notes:		Date Acquired:	Sold on:	Profit:

Brand:	Type:	Model:	Flaws:
Accessories:		Serial:	
Condition:	Color:	Listed: PM ___ EBY ___ MER___ Other:_____	Function:
Category:	Tested:	Cost:	Sold Price:	Loc:	SKU#
Notes:		Date Acquired:	Sold on:	Profit:

Date:_____   # Inventory Log

Brand:	Type:	Model:	Flaws:
Accessories:		Serial:	
Condition:	Color:	Listed: PM ___ EBY ___ MER___ Other:_____	Function:
Category:	Tested:	Cost:	Sold Price:	Loc: SKU#
Notes:		Date Acquired:	Sold on:	Profit:

Brand:	Type:	Model:	Flaws:
Accessories:		Serial:	
Condition:	Color:	Listed: PM ___ EBY ___ MER___ Other:_____	Function:
Category:	Tested:	Cost:	Sold Price:	Loc: SKU#
Notes:		Date Acquired:	Sold on:	Profit:

Brand:	Type:	Model:	Flaws:
Accessories:		Serial:	
Condition:	Color:	Listed: PM ___ EBY ___ MER___ Other:_____	Function:
Category:	Tested:	Cost:	Sold Price:	Loc: SKU#
Notes:		Date Acquired:	Sold on:	Profit:

Brand:	Type:	Model:	Flaws:
Accessories:		Serial:	
Condition:	Color:	Listed: PM ___ EBY ___ MER___ Other:_____	Function:
Category:	Tested:	Cost:	Sold Price:	Loc: SKU#
Notes:		Date Acquired:	Sold on:	Profit:

Date:_____   # Inventory Log

Brand:	Type:	Model:	Flaws:
Accessories:		Serial:	
Condition:	Color:	Listed: PM ___ EBY ___ MER___ Other:_____	Function:
Category:	Tested:	Cost:	Sold Price:	Loc: SKU#
Notes:		Date Acquired:	Sold on:	Profit:

Brand:	Type:	Model:	Flaws:
Accessories:		Serial:	
Condition:	Color:	Listed: PM ___ EBY ___ MER___ Other:_____	Function:
Category:	Tested:	Cost:	Sold Price:	Loc: SKU#
Notes:		Date Acquired:	Sold on:	Profit:

Brand:	Type:	Model:	Flaws:
Accessories:		Serial:	
Condition:	Color:	Listed: PM ___ EBY ___ MER___ Other:_____	Function:
Category:	Tested:	Cost:	Sold Price:	Loc: SKU#
Notes:		Date Acquired:	Sold on:	Profit:

Brand:	Type:	Model:	Flaws:
Accessories:		Serial:	
Condition:	Color:	Listed: PM ___ EBY ___ MER___ Other:_____	Function:
Category:	Tested:	Cost:	Sold Price:	Loc: SKU#
Notes:		Date Acquired:	Sold on:	Profit:

Date:_____ # Inventory Log

Brand:	Type:	Model:	Flaws:
Accessories:		Serial:	
Condition:	Color:	Listed: PM ___ EBY ___ MER___ Other:_____	Function:
Category:	Tested:	Cost:	Sold Price:	Loc: SKU#
Notes:		Date Acquired:	Sold on:	Profit:

Brand:	Type:	Model:	Flaws:
Accessories:		Serial:	
Condition:	Color:	Listed: PM ___ EBY ___ MER___ Other:_____	Function:
Category:	Tested:	Cost:	Sold Price:	Loc: SKU#
Notes:		Date Acquired:	Sold on:	Profit:

Brand:	Type:	Model:	Flaws:
Accessories:		Serial:	
Condition:	Color:	Listed: PM ___ EBY ___ MER___ Other:_____	Function:
Category:	Tested:	Cost:	Sold Price:	Loc: SKU#
Notes:		Date Acquired:	Sold on:	Profit:

Brand:	Type:	Model:	Flaws:
Accessories:		Serial:	
Condition:	Color:	Listed: PM ___ EBY ___ MER___ Other:_____	Function:
Category:	Tested:	Cost:	Sold Price:	Loc: SKU#
Notes:		Date Acquired:	Sold on:	Profit:

Date:_____   # Inventory Log

Brand:	Type:	Model:	Flaws:
Accessories:		Serial:	
Condition:	Color:	Listed: PM ___ EBY ___ MER___ Other:_____	Function:
Category:	Tested:	Cost:	Sold Price:	Loc: SKU#
Notes:		Date Acquired:	Sold on:	Profit:

Brand:	Type:	Model:	Flaws:
Accessories:		Serial:	
Condition:	Color:	Listed: PM ___ EBY ___ MER___ Other:_____	Function:
Category:	Tested:	Cost:	Sold Price:	Loc: SKU#
Notes:		Date Acquired:	Sold on:	Profit:

Brand:	Type:	Model:	Flaws:
Accessories:		Serial:	
Condition:	Color:	Listed: PM ___ EBY ___ MER___ Other:_____	Function:
Category:	Tested:	Cost:	Sold Price:	Loc: SKU#
Notes:		Date Acquired:	Sold on:	Profit:

Brand:	Type:	Model:	Flaws:
Accessories:		Serial:	
Condition:	Color:	Listed: PM ___ EBY ___ MER___ Other:_____	Function:
Category:	Tested:	Cost:	Sold Price:	Loc: SKU#
Notes:		Date Acquired:	Sold on:	Profit:

We hope you enjoyed this book!

Would you please leave us a review on Amazon?

It would really help us out!

Feedback and comments from our readers really make our day!

Thank you!

Queen Thrift

Visit www.QueenThrift.com
For Freebies, Advance Copies, and More!

Are you a Clothing Reseller?

We have an inventory book just for you!

Clothing Reseller Inventory Log Book: Stock Control for Fashion Sellers on Poshmark, eBay, Mercari or Anywhere!

Finally an inventory book for us clothing resellers!

SPACE FOR 696 ITEMS!

The only book you will ever need to keep track of all your items.

How many hours have you spent looking for one or more items in your inventory?

How many orders have you have to cancel because you could not find the item?

Stop wasting money and killing your business, get organized!

The less time you spend figuring out where an item is for sale, the more money you make!

Time is money! That is very true!

This ledger will give you a good view in your inventory. With these inventory sheets you can keep track of your items:

- Cost
- Measurements
- Date acquired
- Store acquired
- Flaws
- Condition
- Location
- This inventory ledger will keep you organized so you have more time to grow your business.

Grab your copy today!

Look for it on Amazon by searching Queen Thrift or

Visit www.QueenThrift.com
Freebies, Advance Copies, and More!

Made in the USA
Columbia, SC
29 June 2025